Essentials of Seamanship
for cruising

Essentials of Seamanship
for cruising

John Watney

CHARTWELL
BOOKS, INC.

Acknowledgements

I owe a great deal to the following skippers for sharing their knowledge with me, and for allowing me to sail with them to obtain most of the photographs in this book. My thanks are also due to their crews who suffered my intrusion on their cruising holidays.

- ☐ Charles Barrington, Director of Seòl Alba, Isle of Skye
- ☐ Cy Blackwell, Director of P & Q Sailing School, Woolverstone
- ☐ Derek Brightwell, skipper of *ITCHEN*
- ☐ John Mills, skipper of *FAIR ENVOY* and Director of Fair Enterprise Sailing, Porthmadog
- ☐ Clive Press, skipper of *SCHEHEREZADE*
- ☐ Mike Tremlett, skipper of *CATSPAW*

I am also indebted to the Royal Yachting Association, the National Sailing Centre at Cowes, the RAF Air-Sea Rescue Service, the Wicklow Sailing Club in Éire and the Scimitar Sailing School at Holyhead for providing me with facilities for photography.

Published by
CHARTWELL BOOKS, INC.
A Division of **BOOK SALES, INC.**
110 Enterprise Avenue
Secaucus, New Jersey 07094

First published in USA in 1980

© John Watney 1980

Published in Great Britain in 1980
by Ward Lock Limited, London,
a Pentos Company.

Designed by Chris Walker
Text filmset in 11/12pt Baskerville 169
by Computer Photoset Ltd., Birmingham

Printed in United States of America

Library of Congress Catalog Card No. 79-57581
ISBN 0-89009-338-5

Contents

Introduction

From the spacious deck of a 6oft converted fishing boat I watched the debris of the Thames float past on the ebb tide towards the open sea. The owner, who was trying to sell the old hulk, must have read my thoughts. 'All you have to do is to start the engine, cast off those ropes, and you can go anywhere in the world. No packing to do, no air fares to pay, no hotels to book—you can go anywhere you like for as long as you like, and take your home with you'.

I went ashore determined to buy his boat and sail round the world with my typewriter—a floating correspondent; that would be the life! He had sold me a dream, but fortunately lack of money and a down-to-earth bank manager prevented him selling me his boat. Some other dreamer bought her, and six months later I read in the newspapers that she had sunk a few miles out of the Thames estuary.

That was my first close encounter with a boat. Eventually I did buy a smaller one which, people said, would take me to the Mediterranean and beyond, and I duly set sail for ever and a day with my typewriter on board. It was not to be for ever. After only a few days I was home again having discovered that while the boat was capable of taking me, I was not capable of taking her.

Twenty years later when I remember that dream it always turns into a nightmare when I think of what might have happened had I gone on. This book is written for those who also dream, but know nothing about boats or sailing. Or, to put it in more prosaic language, those who would like to go cruising but do not know what is involved.

My intention is first to give the novice sufficient background knowledge of boats, how they sail and the language of boating for him to approach the subject objectively as well as romantically. Then to give him a stage-by-stage introduction to the essential skills he will need to acquire before he can become a competent crew member, let alone skipper of his own boat.

If I have made learning seamanship look like hard work I make no apology. The beginner who intends one day to become master of his own yacht and enjoy extended cruising has a lot of study and hard work ahead of him. That sailing is also fun goes without saying, but the fun and the romance increase as growing competence leads to greater achievements. Meanwhile I hope that anyone going for his first sail on a cruising yacht after reading this book will find himself on familiar ground and not feel a complete novice.

Sailing is but one of the pleasures of cruising. To arrive is another, especially when it is at some remote and beautiful place which can only be reached by water where one can marvel at a landscape which the landsman has never seen.

1. Learning to sail

Some theory, especially navigation, can be learnt from books in the comfort of an armchair during winter evenings, and it is certainly worthwhile practising chart work on the dining room table. But learning from books often involves cheating; we tend to absorb what we understand, but ignore what we do not. Reading should supplement the discipline of the classroom—normally night school with the incentive of a final exam. If time or place makes attending night school impossible the next best thing is a recognised correspondence course. That way discipline has to be self-imposed, but at least you get examined even if it is at a distance.

That is only a beginning. It is the practical work and experience which take a lot more time and organising. It is possible to learn by crewing on a friend's boat providing he has more than average competence and is prepared to teach you rather than treat you as a passenger. Unfortunately that does not always work; many an experienced skipper is incapable of imparting his knowledge, or is temperamentally unable to suffer fools gladly—and it is all too easy to make a fool of yourself when you first start working on a sailing boat.

Learning with friends can be a long process. They may not always go sailing when you are free to do so, and vice versa. They may be fair weather sailors who will never take you out in a blow, or they may be very good at handling their boat in any weather once they are at sea, but are quite incompetent when it comes to manoeuvring in a harbour or picking up a mooring.

There are skippers who motor-sail much of the time and use their engines as often as their sails, and have never sailed up to or away from a mooring. Many boats which live in marinas have anchors which their owners do not know how to use.

Sailing with friends like that would leave large gaps in your education and experience. The fact that someone does a lot of sailing does not necessarily prove that he sails well. He may have bad habits with which he has always been lucky enough to get

Opposite In the beginning . . .

away. With him you will learn those same bad habits as well as developing your own.

A lot of family cruising is done in a most dilatory way; nobody wants to get up early to make the best use of tides and, if the wind is not perfect, the engine is started; a log is not kept, and navigation is ignored – all sorts of lazy habits which are not sins if you are only there for the scenery and if the skipper knows the area well, but not much help if you are trying to learn good seamanship.

Many a promising cruise turns out to be a non-event. I was once invited to join a friend and his family on a two-week cruise from Beaulieu on the south coast of England to the Channel Isles and the Brittany coast. I could not go, and fortunately so. They made a one-day hop over to Braye in Alderney where they stayed in the harbour for twelve days, and then sailed home again. And why not? They got what they wanted – a very relaxed holiday. But a novice on that trip would have spent fourteen days to get two days of practical experience.

The quickest and, in the end, the most economic way of learning the essentials of seamanship is to take a practical course at a recognised sailing school. Some of them offer weekend courses for beginners which are useful for those who have family commitments for the annual holiday. Also a weekend on a cruising yacht with a good instructor is a quick and inexpensive way to find out if you really do want to take up sailing. Many a person with romantic notions about sailing has found after one day at sea that he hates it – especially if he spent the day being seasick.

A weekend course is also a useful preliminary to a full week or fortnight on a coastal cruising course. Your fellow students may not be complete novices and a little previous experience does help to bridge the gap between their apparent competence and your feeling of incompetence. In truth if the instructor is worth his salt, and if your heart is in the business, you may find that you are very soon doing as well as anybody else.

A week is the least time that is of any real value because there is so much more to seamanship than pulling ropes and holding the tiller – things which can only be learnt by eating and sleeping, living and working together as a team in a small space at sea. As well, a night passage which involves getting out of a warm bunk in the middle of the night to keep watch in a cold cockpit with salt spray stinging your eyes will show you the other side of the coin.

A week or two of cruising under instruction, especially if you are lucky enough to get some strong winds and a little bad weather, but with a skipper who keeps on sailing and making you work, is worth a couple of years of day-sailing in fair weather with your friends.

Classroom instruction at the
National Sailing Centre,
Cowes, Isle of Wight.

A family do their theory in the
cockpit before starting a
practical sailing course.

A novice crew learning the ropes.

A one-week or two-week coastal cruising course under a good instructor should be sufficient experience to enable you to be a useful crew member on any cruising boat. Whether it is enough experience to enable you to be the skipper of your own boat will depend on how competent your own crew is and what type of cruising you intend doing.

In some countries the decision is not left to the boat owner. He has to pass tests before he is allowed to take charge of a boat, and even then his sailing range is dictated by a number of grades for which he has to qualify.

In Britain there are at present no restrictions, but there is a voluntary scheme of cruising courses for a range of certificates which are awarded by the Royal Yachting Association. Although optional, their certificates are a very valuable indicator of competence to anyone who intends to take his sailing seriously and reach a high standard of seamanship.

The lowest grade is the RYA Competent Crew Certificate, for which it is necessary to have satisfactorily completed a shore-based course in seamanship, navigation and meteorology, and practical sailing instruction including a minimum of 100 miles with four hours of night sailing. To qualify for the grade of RYA Day Skipper Certificate the sea time must cover 15 days, 200

A novice crew starting off on a weekend course.

miles, and eight hours of night sailing. There is no examination for those grades, which are awarded at the discretion of RYA Instructors. To qualify for the RYA DoT Coastal Skipper Certificate requires taking a full course on navigation, and the sea time is increased to 300 miles and twelve night hours followed by an oral examination.

The grade which should be the ambition of every serious cruising skipper is the RYA/DoT Yachtmaster Offshore Certificate for which a great deal of theoretical and practical knowledge has to be acquired, plus 50 days of sea time covering a minimum of 2,500 miles with five passages of over 60 miles, two as a skipper and two overnight. There is then a stiff oral examination.

It would be very exceptional for anybody to progress from novice to Yachtmaster in under two years, even if he spent four or five weeks sailing under instruction and worked hard and continuously at his theory.

There is one further grade, RYA/DoT Yachtmaster Ocean, which can only be reached after qualifying for Yachtmaster Offshore and it includes making a 500-mile non-stop passage and the use of the sextant for taking sights at sea. Only RYA qualified instructors and recognised schools can operate the scheme and grant certificates.

There is no doubt that the best way to ensure that you learn your seamanship the right way without leaving any important gaps in your knowledge and experience is to combine sailing for pleasure with sailing under instruction to get your RYA Certificates up to Yachtmaster.

However, those Certificates should not be considered as an end in themselves, but only as proof to yourself that you have reached the minimal degree of competence at each stage.

Ideally you should wait until you have attained your RYA Coastal Skipper Certificate before becoming master of your own yacht. But all work and no play makes Jack a dull boy, and there is no reason why you should not enjoy sailing your own boat within the limits of your increasing competence and confidence in the meanwhile.

In the U.S. hundreds of local schools and clubs give private classes in all facets of boating. The U.S. Power Squadron has more than 400 local units which present free to the public a 10-lesson course in basic boating safety, as well as advanced instruction courses to its members. The Coast Guard offers a correspondence 'skipper's course' and the Coast Guard auxiliary sponsors a number of courses in boating safety for the public, In addition, the American Red Cross conduct small-boat safety classes.

A good way of combining pleasure with learning is to go cruising on a charter yacht with a skipper who is also a qualified instructor. You can either make up your own party with family and friends to share the cost, or take pot luck and join a crew of unknown individuals.

Then as a charterer rather than a pupil you and the rest of the crew will be able to decide the pace and destination of the cruise and take your turn as navigator, helmsman and acting skipper with a professional on hand to give advice and correct your faults.

Chartering is not quite the same as owning your own boat, but–unless money is no object–it enables you to sail bigger and better boats than you could afford to buy and maintain, at a fraction of the cost. It also enables you to get experience on a variety of boats in different sailing waters before finally deciding the type of boat and cruising area which best suit your temperament and capabilities.

Perhaps the most enjoyable way for a beginner to gain experience and confidence is to take a short three-day practical course at a recognised school to learn how to steer a boat and help with the sails, and then go flotilla sailing in the nice warm waters of the Mediterranean. Cruising in company, or flotilla sailing, is a relaxed form of sailing holiday which has developed over the last few years. Instead of being trapped on a boat with an instructor, you are left to your own devices except that you cruise together in a fleet. Even if as a family or party of friends you take over a whole boat and not one of you knows much about sailing, you are all the time within sight and sound of the other boats and helpful advice if you get in a tangle. A flotilla leader on a yacht with an experienced crew will point the direction according to the wind and destination, and will come alongside if you are having real trouble. If the worst comes to the worst you will get a tow to the next picnic bay or fishing harbour.

The sun is guaranteed, the water is warm, there are no tides, and the leader of the fleet knows all about the local winds and the safe route to take from point to point, so you can concentrate on the practical job of making the boat sail. Do not be put off by the idea of spending a week or a fortnight playing follow-my-leader. If you are confident enough you can peel off and do your own thing within certain limits and rejoin the fleet at the end of the day.

You will certainly not be sailing in company with beginners only. These holidays have become an economic alternative to the responsibility of running their own boats in less pleasant climates for many very experienced yachtsmen. Some of the fleets include a number of performance cruiser/racers to satisfy such sailors. So you can sail with and talk to people with a wide range of experience, and have a lovely holiday–far better than one spent flogging around in the cold grey waters of the northern hemisphere during a summer that has failed to materialise.

If the possibility of owning your own cruising yacht–for family or financial reasons–is still several years away, you might consider taking up dinghy sailing in the meantime. There is no better way of learning the art of sailing than to sail a dinghy competitively. Many of the best ocean racing crews were successful dinghy sailors first. Anybody who has mastered the techniques of making a dinghy sail well in all conditions is unlikely to have difficulty adapting to a larger yacht. What he will still have to learn is the seamanship and navigational skills which apply to a big boat which he will not have had to use while sailing a dinghy in his familiar home waters.

2. A sailing boat is a wind machine

This square-rigged beach toy inflatable boat illustrates the most primitive type of sail. The 'helmsman' is trimming the sail to the wind by two ropes (braces) attached to the outer ends of the yard. Being flat bottomed, the inflatable boat is as likely to sail sideways as forwards. The crew is trying to achieve some directional stability by using a paddle as a leeboard to stop sideways drift.

It is easy to comprehend how a boat can sail in the same direction as the wind; any floating object—an empty box for example—will be blown downwind. But that is not how boats sail most of the time. Watch them racing round the buoys, or coming and going in opposite directions at the entrance to a harbour. You will see them sailing in all different directions at the same time—downwind, obliquely to the wind, across the wind and even apparently into the wind. How do they do it? How can a boat sail against the very wind which drives it?

The theory can be explained in terms of aerodynamics, hydrodynamics and parallelograms of force, but theory is not much help when one is first confronted by a maze of wires, ropes, sails and other gear on a sailing boat. It seems more practical to explain what actually happens and what can be observed rather than dwell on the abstract.

A boat set adrift in a breeze is like an empty box; she will drift downwind (at this stage the effect of any tide or current can be ignored), but she will also be blown sideways because the side of the boat facing the wind will act as a sail. Obviously a flat-bottomed boat will be blown faster across the top of the water than one with a deeply immersed hull or a deep keel which will resist the lateral movement through the water.

Now if a very simple sail is set—a square or rectangle of canvas or other material on a pole hung at right angles to the mast—the wind will catch that sail and, provided it is big enough, the boat will sail quite efficiently, but only if she is steered downwind as in the photograph.

Such a crude sailing rig is, therefore, unworkable although something similar was surely used by primitive peoples to blow them across water when the wind served.

Many thousands of years ago it was discovered that matters could be greatly improved by arranging a sail in such a way that its angle could be altered relative to the wind direction.

Running before the wind the yards on the square-rigged Sail Training Ship *Royalist* are set at right angles to her fore and aft line.

With ropes attached to the four corners of the sail it was not only possible to alter the angle of the sail across the boat, but, by shortening or lengthening the ropes, the shape of the sail could be altered to hold more wind or to spill wind when it blew too strong.

With that rig a boat could be sailed with the wind blowing a little from one side by altering the angle of the sail so that it continued to fill while, at the same time, holding the head of the boat on a course at an angle to the wind with the aid of a rudder.

A rudder in its simplest form is a flat piece of wood or metal hinged to the back of the boat which can be turned to the left or right by means of a lever, which is called a tiller. As long as a rudder is held straight in line with the centre line of the boat, water will flow unimpeded either side of it.

As soon as it is turned in one direction or the other, it will interrupt the flow of water on one side which will build up a pressure against its flat surface. That pressure will try to push the rudder back straight, but if the tiller is being held firmly the rudder will not move, and so the pressure of the water is transmitted to the boat and the back, or stern, is pushed away instead of the rudder blade. Now because a boat pivots on a point about its centre, the head or bows of the boat will be turned in the opposite direction to the stern. That is how a boat is steered.

It is well worth remembering when it comes to manoeuvring a boat that she always turns on a point and not in an arc like a motor car. The point on which she turns varies from boat to boat, but is approximately one-third of the waterline length back from the bow when moving forwards, and one-third of the waterline length from the stern when going astern. If the boat is stationary she will pivot on a point near her centre. It is also worth remembering that a tiller is a lever. It is, therefore, always moved in the opposite direction to the way you want the head of the boat to move or, if you are looking backwards, in the same direction as you want the stern to move. When going in reverse— which is called going astern in a boat—the tiller must be moved in the opposite direction to the way the stern of the boat must go and in the same direction as the bows.

The square sail in its basic form is a limited rig because it has very limited ability to drive a boat to windward, and the round hulled boats on which it was first used lost a lot of ground sideways. It stands to reason that if a boat is trying to go forward but the wind is blowing from one side, it will try to push the boat sideways.

It is only the resistance of the hull in the water which prevents it from being completely successful, and the resulting forward motion is a compromise between the two forces; the boat moves in a crab fashion—the head points one way, but her actual track

The flags on top of the masts of this brigantine show that the wind is coming from just forward of the beam and the boat is, therefore, sailing a little into the wind. The square sails have been trimmed to a fore and aft position. A brigantine is a two-masted vessel which carries a gaff-rigged mainsail, fore and aft headsails, and square sails on her foremast only.

The leeboard of a sailing barge.

over the ground is at an angle downwind. This is called leeway. The side of the boat facing the wind is called the windward or weather side, and the other side, which is facing away from the wind, is the leeward side.

There are two ways to reduce the amount of leeway a boat will make; one is to hang a large flat board over her lee side (leeboard) in the manner of a Dutch or Thames sailing barge, the other is to extend the bottom of the boat in the form of a projecting keel. Either way you get a flat surface pressing against the water and resisting the sideways motion. The bows of the boat are shaped to offer the minimum resistance to the water, so it takes less force to push the boat forward than it does to push it sideways.

There is a risk, however, that if the boat is carrying too much sail for the strength of the wind the sideways-acting pressure of the wind, frustrated in its efforts to push the boat sideways, will expend its energy in pushing the boat over on its side. In other words, the boat will heel over. As the boat heels over the drag of the hull through the water increases and the boat slows down.

If the keel is big enough and heavy enough it will act as a counterweight to the heeling movement and keep the boat upright, or nearly upright. But that is something which developed quite late in the history of boat design and will be explained later in this section.

It might now seem that the square sail can only be used for sailing off the wind – that is with the wind coming from anywhere behind the boat. That is not quite true. It is possible to sail a few degrees into the wind if a square sail is trimmed almost flat in a near fore-and-aft position. If it were not so the early navigators would never have achieved the voyages they did and returned home.

Certainly they knew how to do this, even if they did not understand what made it possible. In fact, although sail design was developed more and more over the centuries to enable ships to sail to windward, the mystery of how a boat can sail against the wind which drives her was not fully understood until the arrival of the aeroplane.

What makes an aeroplane fly? Not air under the wings lifting it up, as was once believed, but suction on the top of the wings. When an aeroplane taxies along the ground it creates an air flow past its wings. This air flow passes unimpeded below the wings, but the air going over the top of the wings is deflected by the curve of the leading edges and has to travel faster. This causes a partial vacuum on the upper surface of the wings. A partial vacuum means a lower air pressure, and it is the differential pressure above and below the wings which 'sucks' the wings upwards and lifts the aeroplane off the ground. If an aeroplane wing is turned

into the vertical position it can be likened to a rigid sail. And a sail correctly trimmed can be likened to a thin aeroplane wing. When the wind blows past its two surfaces a differential pressure is set up which 'sucks' the leeward side of the sail forwards. That, in very simple terms, is how a boat can be made to sail to windward. There are, of course, other factors involved which will be explained in due course.

It was to make sails take on what is now known as an aerofoil shape, so that they would drive a boat to windward, that the fore-and-aft rig was developed and has now almost entirely taken over from the square rig – although the two are still sometimes used together, particularly on sail-training ships. One of the earliest attempts at the fore-and-aft concept was the Arab dhow. The various forms of lugsail rigs are in the same genre.

It is the front third area of a sail which produces most of the driving force, and up to at least 70 per cent of that force is derived from the low pressure on its leeward side provided a good aerofoil shape is maintained.

It is, therefore, important that both the leading edge of a sail, called the luff, and the shape of its front area should allow a smooth flow of air. This is best achieved with sails which have a luff that is tensioned, which is why nearly all sails are attached along their leading edge to either a mast or a stay.

Left The venturi, or 'slot', is between the dark mainsail and the light headsail. The boat is on a close reach and, therefore, the direction of the wind will be from about 45° on the port bow. But the flag flying from the crosstree shows that the wind in the slot is being directed along the fore and aft face of the mainsail.
Right The slot between genoa and mainsail seen from up forward on a 30 ft (9 m) cruising boat close hauled on the port tack. The ensign on the stern pointing over the starboard quarter shows that the direction of the apparent wind is approximately 45° to the heading of the boat, whereas the courtesy flag below the crosstree is pointing fore and aft showing that the wind is being directed through the slot onto the leeward side of the aerofoil-shaped mainsail.

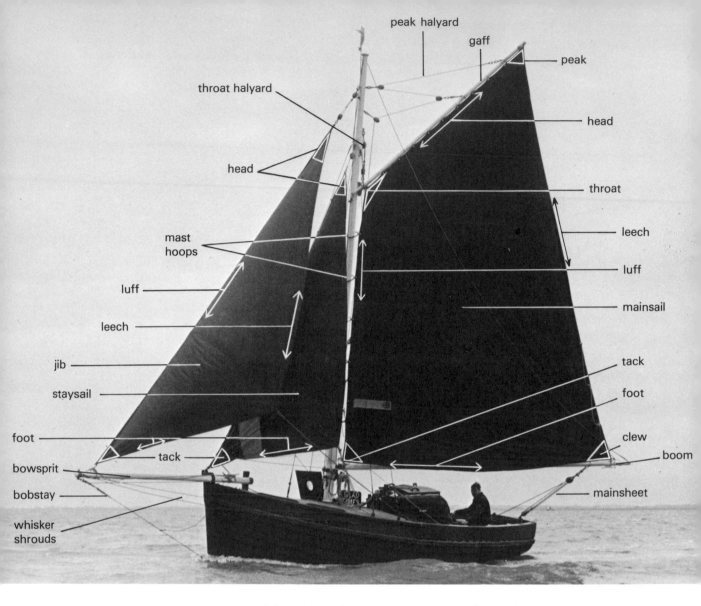

peak halyard

gaff

peak

throat halyard

head

head

throat

mast hoops

leech

luff

luff

mainsail

leech

tack

jib

foot

staysail

foot

clew

tack

boom

bowsprit

bobstay

mainsheet

whisker shrouds

A gaff rigged cutter.

Most boats have two or more sails, and where one overlaps another the slot between the two forms a venturi which accelerates the flow of air round the leeward side of the sail behind it, further reducing the pressure and thus increasing its driving force.

The first true fore-and-aft rig, which has been with us now for several hundred years, is the gaff rig. It has a foursided sail hoisted behind the mast and attached to it by hoops. It is held in shape by a spar along its top edge—the gaff—and another at the bottom—the boom, both of which swivel on the mast. A smaller triangular sail is hoisted on a stay forward of the mast.

It is a good working rig for boats whose owners are not worried by a modest windward performance compared to the bermudan rig (called marconi rig in America) which, in one form or another, is common to most modern yachts.

The high narrow bermudan sail plan has a long leading edge or luff which gives it more drive to windward than the gaff with its relatively short luff. A bermudan sail can also hold a much better shape than a gaff with its heavy spar at the top which tends to sag to leeway underway.

Before dealing with the other factors which contribute to the sailing abilities of a boat it would be well to run through the proper names and items of gear before they become too numerous to remember.

Going back to the square rig: the spar at right angles to the mast to which the sail is attached is called a yard, and the rope or wire which is used to haul it up into position is a halyard (haul yard). It is a name which is applied universally to any rope or wire which is used for hoisting and lowering a sail, spar, flag or other object.

The ropes which are used to trim the sails are called sheets, and they are attached to the corners, or clews, of the sail. On a fore-and-aft sail there is only one clew—the aft corner to which the sheets are attached. The holes or eyes in a sail to which ropes are attached are cringles.

If the mast is unsupported it is said to be unstayed. If it is stayed then the wires or ropes preventing it from falling forwards or backwards are called forestays or backstays respectively, while those that prevent it from falling sideways are called shrouds. All these wires are collectively known as the standing rigging.

The running rigging consists of the sheets, halyards and other movable wires and ropes used to set up and trim the sails.

So far these names apply to all sailing rigs. A square sail rig may have several sails—big ships had up to 26 set on three masts—all of them with different names, but in this context they are only of academic interest.

A fore-and-aft rig can also have many different sails set on more than one mast, but the most common combination these days is the sloop rig. This is one mast with two sails—a mainsail behind (abaft) the mast, and a headsail, or jib, which is a triangular sail set up on the forestay running from the top or near top of the mast to the bows. On some boats a spar called a bowsprit is rigged, projecting from the bow with a forestay going to its outer end to carry the headsail.

A headsail is set with the narrowest point of the triangle at the top, which is called the head of the sail. The leading edge, the luff, is attached at intervals along its length to the forestay. The bottom corner of the luff is attached to a fixing at the bow. It is tacked down, as it were, and that corner is called the tack.

The halyard attached to the head of the sail is used to haul the luff taut. The bottom edge which runs roughly parallel to the

head

batten

batten

luff

leech

mainsail

clew

mainsheet

jib or
headsail

leech

luff

tack

foot

A bermudan sloop close hauled.

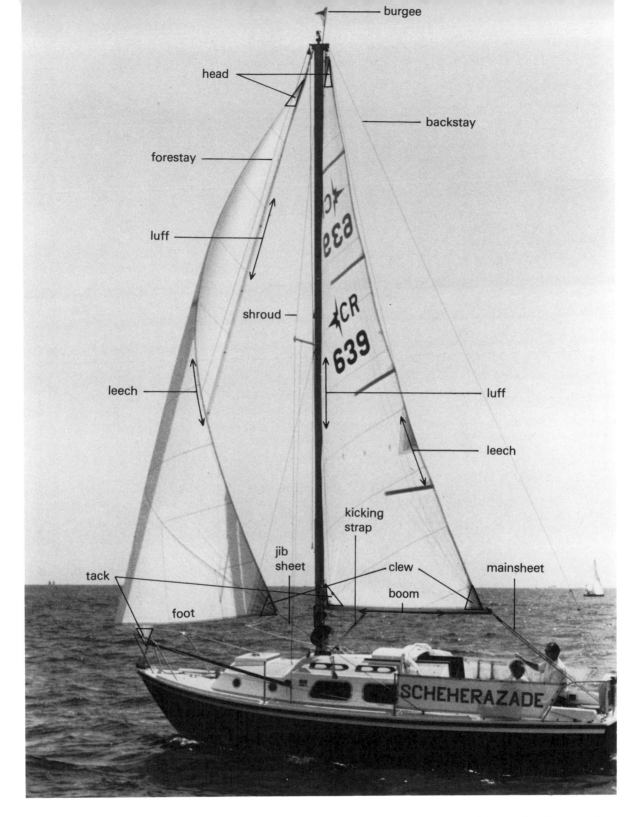

burgee

head

backstay

forestay

luff

shroud

leech

luff

leech

kicking
strap

jib
sheet

clew

mainsheet

tack

boom

foot

SCHEHERAZADE

A bermudan sloop running.

deck is the foot, and the after edge from the foot to the head is the leech. An odd name. Think of the *leech* as the *lee*ward edge of the sail to help you remember. The corner between the foot and the leech is the clew to which the sheets are attached to control the sail. If you haven't a clew you can't control the sail!

A bermudan mainsail has the same parts as a headsail, but a gaff mainsail is more complicated. It has four sides and the whole length of the top side, which is laced to the gaff, is called the head. The point at the outer end of the gaff—which would be the head on a triangular sail—is the peak and it sticks up in the air like one. The other corner where the gaff meets the mast is the throat; easy to remember because it is at the end of the gaff by the jaws which engage on the mast.

The foot of a mainsail—gaff or bermudan—is attached to the boom at the tack and the clew, and along its length either by rope lacing or slides sewn onto the sail and running in a track on the boom. Sometimes the sail is loose-footed—being attached only at the tack and clew, but it is a rare arrangement.

A mainsail is hoisted and lowered by a halyard which is hand-hauled or winched (depending on its size) to keep the luff taut. The luff on modern yachts is held in a track or groove in the mast so that it is not only tensioned by the halyard, but is also kept flat by being held onto the mast.

The mainsheet, which is used to control the mainsail, does not go onto the clew itself but to a fixing on the outer end of the boom to which the clew is also attached. So the position of the sail is controlled by moving the boom. To help it keep a regular flat unbroken curve, thin battens made of flexible strips of wood or plastic, are slid into pockets at intervals up the after-edge of the sail to stop the leech from curling inwards and spoiling the shape.

The shape that a sail takes up, and therefore how effective it is, depends in the first instance on its design and how well it has been cut by the sailmaker. A bermudan sail may appear to have a straight luff and foot because one is attached to a straight mast and the other to a straight boom. But in fact they are both cut on a curve so that when the sail fills it takes up a good aerofoil shape. A badly-made sail will never set well, nor will one which has been badly treated or stretched out of shape.

The sloop rig is not only the commonest, but also the simplest, of rigs with its large mainsail and a single headsail. It is easy to handle on medium-sized boats, and because it requires the mast to be stepped forward of the centre of the boat it leaves room for a relatively large main cabin below.

Returning to the subject of how a boat sails, it is not enough to understand the aerodynamic function of the sails and leave it at that. On their own they would not drive a boat forward except when the wind was behind her. In that situation the force of the wind is blowing in the direction of the bows, and the sails are trimmed almost at right angles to the boat's centre line, to catch the wind. Everything is in favour of her moving forwards.

But when she is sailing on other courses with the wind blowing from one side or in front she has to rely on the low pressure on the leeward sides of her sails for most of her driving force. That force does not act in a forward direction, but at right angles to the chord of the curve of the sail. So, whatever the angle of the sails, the boat is being pulled to a greater or lesser degree sideways. Therefore the tendency is for the boat to sail sideways, to make leeway.

The hull of the boat produces some resistance to this sideways movement, but the most effective resistance comes from the keel which acts in the water in a somewhat similar way to a sail in the air: a fluid—air—flows over the surface of a sail; the surface of a keel moves through a fluid—water.

When a boat makes leeway she moves sideways at an angle, and the keel sets up a force in reaction which counteracts the angle of leeway. The forces acting on the keel have a far greater effect on a far smaller area than those acting on the larger area of a sail. This is because the keel is rigid and water is almost 800 times denser than air. The effectiveness of a keel is, of course, proportional to its surface, but it is also proportional to the square of the speed of the boat. So the faster a boat sails the less way she will lose to leeward.

To put it all together simply: there is a force trying to drive the boat sideways, and an opposite force trying to resist that movement. The shape of the boat makes it difficult for her to move sideways, but easy for her to slip through the water forwards, and the interaction of the two forces ends up by driving her forwards.

All boats make some leeway when sailing into the wind; how much depends on the balance between the design of the hull and keel and the sail plan. How well a boat will sail to windward, and how close to the wind without making a lot of leeway, depends first on her designer, builder and sailmaker. After that it is up to the people who sail her.

When a boat is sailing there is a constant tug-o'-war going on between the aerodynamic force above the water pulling her one way and the hydrodynamic force under the water pulling her the other way. If she is to sail in a straight line at a constant speed the two forces must be balanced and pull against each other along the same axis.

If the aerodynamic force from the sails were centred near the front of the boat, and if the hydrodynamic force from the keel

When a boat is heeled over her waterline length is increased.

were centred near the back of the boat, she would spin round out of control. But if both forces are exerted from the same point on the boat she will not be pulled more one way than the other and will be able to keep going in a straight line.

The aerodynamic force is said to act through a point called the Centre of Effort (CE), and the hydrodynamic force through the Centre of Lateral Resistance (CLR).

The CE is a point in a sail plan through which the combined wind forces are calculated to act. The CLR is the point about which a boat turns or pivots. If the CE and the CLR are aligned the boat is perfectly balanced and, theoretically, will sail herself in a straight line without the help of her rudder. It is a very rare state of affairs, and not entirely practical.

Normally the CLR lies just in front of the CE so that the opposing forces tend to turn the bows towards the wind and the stern away from it. This is called weather helm and, in moderation, is a good thing. It means that the helmsman has to put a slight pressure on the tiller to correct the tendency of the boat to turn up into the wind and so he keeps a feel of the boat.

To counteract too much weather helm the rudder has to be kept so far over that it acts as a brake and slows the boat down. It is also very tiring for the helmsman. If the positions of the two centres are reversed and the CLR lies just behind the CE the boat will carry lee helm, which means she will have a tendency to bear away from the wind all the time.

When a boat is upright and wearing her normal working sails the overall balance between hull and rig may be correct, but when she starts sailing there are many factors which can upset that balance. For instance, when she heels—as she will when pressed to sail into the wind—the shape of that part of the hull immersed in the water will change the CLR, she will almost certainly slow down, and the CE will move to leeward producing a torque which will increase weather helm and there will be a tendency for the boat to luff up into the wind if the helm is not held firmly.

When sails are changed or reefed—made smaller by folding or rolling, as they have to be to suit increased wind force—the CE changes considerably. If the relative size of the headsail is increased because the mainsail is reefed, the CE moves well forward, but if the headsail is taken off and the boat sails with the mainsail only, then the CE moves aft. The CE also moves to and fro if one sail is hauled in fairly flat and the other is allowed to belly out.

The way in which a boat is loaded affects her trim; if she is stern heavy or bow heavy the point on which she turns changes and so, therefore, does the CLR.

These are just some of the factors which affect the balance of a boat, and their effect will differ from one boat to another. The small amount of imbalance which a boat will nearly always have can be counteracted by the tiller and by trimming the sails to match the force and direction of the wind and the speed of the boat. Any major imbalance means changing the sail plan and/or the trim of the boat herself.

Sensing the balance of a boat, and keeping her trimmed and sailing well in varying conditions, are part of the art of seamanship. Once you understand what happens it is then a question of feel or sensitivity which some people acquire more quickly than others, but it will only come with practice.

The terms 'downwind' and 'into the wind' which have been used up to now for the sake of simplicity are too broad in meaning to be used when discussing the finer points of sailing.

A boat sailing with her main well reefed in a strong wind.

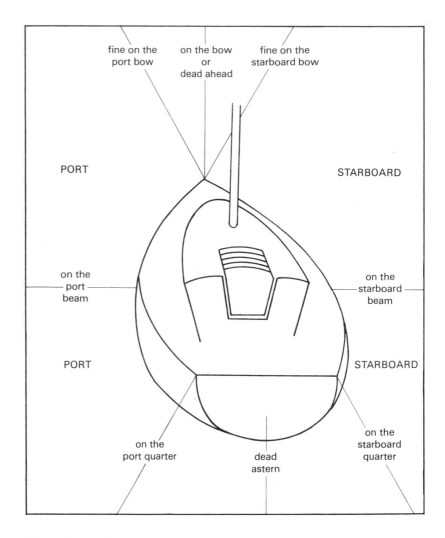

Port and starboard.

At this stage a few more nautical words need to be introduced, and the most important are 'port' and 'starboard'. They are the most overworked but necessary words in the nautical vocabulary.

Port means left. The left side of the boat is always its port side and it does not change, whether you are looking forward or aft. When standing at the stern and looking towards the bows everything on *your* left hand is on the boat's port hand. And that will remain the port-hand side even when you are facing aft and it is on your right hand.

Anything just ahead of and a little to the left of the boat is said to be on the port bow. If it is directly ahead it is on the bow.

Anything seen over the aft left-hand section of the boat is on the port quarter. If it is directly behind the boat it is astern.

Starboard means right, and it is used in the same way–starboard side, starboard hand, starboard bow, etc. At night you can tell which side of a boat or ship you are looking at because it will carry a red light on its port side and a green light on its starboard side. If you can see both get out of the way!

When a boat turns it does so to port or to starboard, not to the left or to the right. But the direction in which a boat is going relative to the wind direction is called the port or starboard tack. It takes its name from the direction *from* which the wind is blowing, or the side of the boat *over* which the wind is blowing.

If sailing on the starboard tack the wind is blowing on your starboard side, but if you turn to starboard (approximately 90°) the wind will then be on your port side and so the boat will be on a port tack although she has turned to starboard.

The verb 'to tack' also refers to the action of changing direction by turning a boat 90° through the wind so that she changes from a port to a starboard tack, and vice versa. You will remember that the lower fore corner of a sail is called the tack. It is the point at which a sail is attached to the fore end of the boom or to the bows so it always remains amidships and does not move when the boat tacks. The language can be very perverse!

The points of sailing are divided into four directions on each tack–port and starboard–plus the point when the wind is dead astern. There is also a neutral position in which a boat will not sail at all, that is when the wind is dead ahead. In that position the wind blows along both sides of the sails which shake and flap like washing on a line with no effect on the boat except that it may be blown backwards by its own windage. The average boat will not sail closer than about 45° to the wind, although some high performance racing yachts can get as close as 35° with a skillful crew.

A boat must, therefore, turn about 45° away from the wind before her sails will start to work. She is then sailing 'close hauled' and the sails will be sheeted in (hauled in by their sheets) hard. This is the point of sailing which looks most spectacular as the boat heels over and, because she is sailing into the wind, spray will fly off the bows. But in fact it requires a great deal of finesse to balance the boat, it puts a strain on both crew and gear, and in the end the boat does not move as fast as she will on other points of sailing. She will also make leeway.

Turning further away from the wind until it is at an angle of 50° to 60° to the boat's direction of travel the sails are let out a little and the angle of heel may decrease if the wind is not too strong. The boat is now on a 'close reach'. She is still going to windward, but the wind is only just ahead.

Close hauled on the port tack. The helmsman on the weather side of the cockpit has the tiller well up, indicating some weather helm.

From a close reach the boat bears away to a 'beam reach', when the wind is at right angles to the boat and blowing on her beam. This is a pleasant point of sailing. The boat goes faster, the sails are at an angle of about 45° to the line of the boat, and there should be hardly any pressure on the tiller so the helmsman can relax a little. It is a good time for going below and putting on the kettle.

A 'broad reach' is when the wind is blowing from over one quarter, in other words still from one side but also a little over the stern. The sails are let well out and the boat is sailing well before the wind. The helmsman has to concentrate more to keep a steady course, but the crew will hardly feel the wind which is now moving in approximately the same direction as the boat. It is the time to undo oilies and feel the warmth of the sun, if there is any.

Finally there is 'running' when the wind is blowing from dead astern. The sails are trimmed out at almost right angles to the boat and the sense of speed is reduced because the wind and the

Cruising in company downwind. The boat in the foreground has her spinnaker up and her genoa is lying ready for hoisting on the foredeck. The other boat has set a cruising chute to starboard and her jib is goosewinged out on a whisker pole to port.

boat are both moving in the same direction. Unless the wind direction remains constant, the helmsman has to concentrate very hard to keep the boat dead before the wind otherwise the wind will get round behind the sails and the boom will crash across from one side of the boat to the other. It is called an 'accidental gybe', and God help anybody whose head is in the way.

The same problem arises if there is a heavy or lumpy sea which can throw the boat off course. Running is a point of sailing much enjoyed by those off watch after a spell of wet sailing to windward at a sickening angle of heel, but, except in light airs and a calm sea, it demands constant watchfulness by the crew.

The point on which a boat is sailed will depend on a combination of factors, voluntary and involuntary. Most boats perform better on one point of sailing than on others, and the skipper who is sailing for fun rather than to reach a fixed destination will try and keep on the one which gives him the best sail, for as long as possible.

He may change the point of sailing for one of many reasons: to make the boat go faster, to give the crew a rest after a hard thrash to windward, to bring the boat on an even keel for a while so that food can be prepared or, in the case of a run downwind, to enjoy the warmth of the sun without the cold of the wind. If he wants to reef or change sail he will bring the boat close to the wind to allow pressure to be reduced from the sails so that they can be hoisted and lowered, and at the same time the speed of the boat is reduced so that conditions for working on deck are safer.

But very often there is no choice. If the boat has to pass between or go round hazards, clear a point of land, get out of the way of shipping, run for shelter before a storm, or if time is pressing and a destination has to be reached, then the course which has to be set and the direction and strength of the wind at the time will dictate the point of sailing. If it means a wet, uncomfortable sail or a slow and sluggish performance, or even a seasick-making motion, there is often nothing that can be done about it. Sailing cannot always be pleasant and comfortable; but the times when it is not are usually the most exhilarating.

The moment a boat moves she creates her own wind which increases in strength with her speed, so it has neither the same strength nor the same direction as the true wind. It is called the relative wind and it combines with the true wind to become the apparent wind, which is the wind which is felt by the crew and acts on the sails.

The direction of the apparent wind, and to some extent its force, can be judged by looking at the burgee on the top of the mast. If this is not immediately understood think of a motor car with a flag on its bonnet. The car is stationary and a gentle breeze is blowing across the road from right to left. The flag will blow out at right angles to the car, pointing to the left.

The car then starts to move, and by the time it is going at 20 miles an hour the flag will be blowing right down the centre line of the car towards the windscreen. Apparently the wind has gone round from one side to the front of the car.

The same thing happens with a moving boat—the apparent wind is always ahead of the true wind (nearer the bows), except of course when running with the wind aft, and the faster the boat moves the further ahead the wind moves and the stronger it becomes. This is why one sees the phenomenon of a boat sailing with its burgee streaming aft giving the impression that she is sailing directly into the face of the wind which is driving her forwards.

3. There is no such thing as a perfect boat

THE HULL

At one time there was little difference between the small cruising yacht and the fishing or work boat from which she was derived. All boats were built of wood, and the belief was that weight meant strength which, in many ways, it did. The old fashioned way of building relied on timbers of relatively very large size so that even if half the boat rotted away there was still enough left to keep her afloat.

To drive such a heavy object through the water required equally heavy sails and gear and, therefore, a lot of man power and muscle power to handle them.

With the coming of plywood, moulded wood, light alloys and plastics it became possible to achieve strength with lightness. There are still heavy displacement boats built, although not as heavy as were the old timers. If they have any advantages over the modern light displacement boats they are mainly psychological– a continuing belief that weight means strength.

They do tend to be a bit more comfortable in rough going because their inertia in the water gives them a gentler motion, but performance in light winds is always poor.

The modern light displacement hull comes in two basic configurations: the long keel on a curved bottom, and the fin keel on an almost flat bottom.

The long keel has one undoubted advantage–it allows a boat to take the ground easily, although of course she has to be propped up against a harbour wall or something. It also has the reputation of giving a boat more directional stability than a fin keel. People say about their long keel boats that, once the sails are properly trimmed, the boat will sail herself and that the helm can be left for short periods without the boat wandering off course.

The truth is that a boat with a narrow fin keel can be just as easy to steer, but only if she is perfectly balanced, but is unlikely

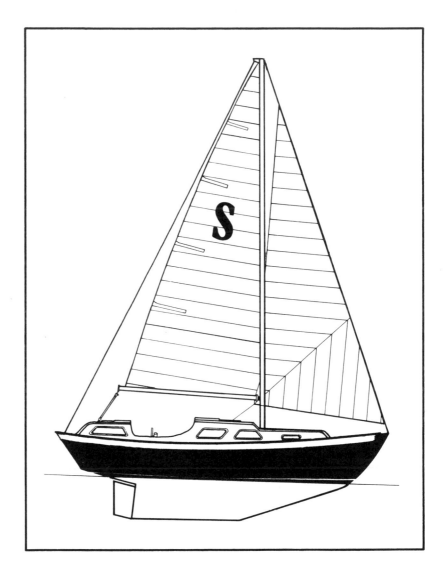

The Samphire 29, a
traditionally designed cruising
yacht with a long keel.

to sail herself. The popularity of the long keel for cruising boats
stems from the fact that they do not have to be quite as perfectly
balanced as a fin keel boat to keep reasonable directional stability.

The rudder on a long keel boat is at the end of the keel and is,
therefore, working in disturbed water which reduces its efficiency.
On a fin keel boat the rudder is hung aft at a distance from the
keel and so works in less disturbed water and, being further away
from the keel, it has a greater leverage and so may need less
effort to turn it.

Normally a rudder is hinged to a skeg, which is like an embryonic keel of its own. This gives it good support and reasonable

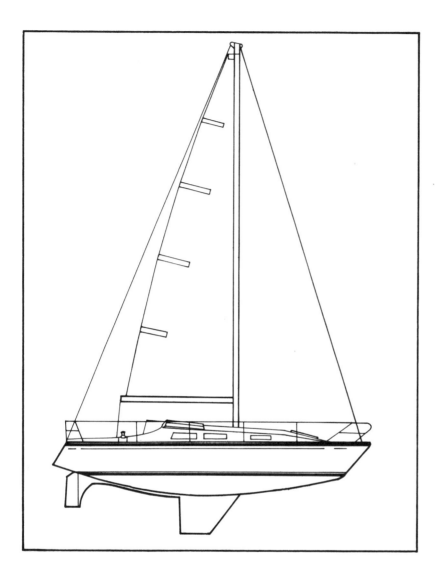

The Quicksilver 30 cruiser racer with fin keel and rudder aft on a skeg.

protection against any underwater obstruction. More sensitive, but now less popular, are balanced rudders which are hung on their own supported only by their stock which has to take all the strain. These are particularly vulnerable in gale conditions when the forces imposed on them can bend or break the stock.

There is less chance of a boat with a balanced rudder steering herself without a hand on the helm, and the extreme sensitivity of such rudders requires equal sensitivity and concentration on the part of the helmsman. A beginner would probably be unhappy trying to control a boat with a balanced rudder; he needs to practise first on something less lively.

The long keeled boat is slower to answer the helm and less manoeuvrable in a confined space than the fin keel boat with her rudder separate at the stern. The light displacement fin keeler will turn on the proverbial sixpence and will respond much faster even when carrying a reduced sail area.

On the whole, the long keel, slightly heavier, boat is probably a safer bet for the inexperienced because she will take more kindly to being unbalanced and to poor sail trimming. The modern light displacement performance boat is much more susceptible to sail trim and, unless the owner knows how to handle her, she will behave badly.

In recent years there has been an increasing trend towards beamier boats, so much so that, from some angles of view, they look almost as wide as they are long. It is a development which has come from the rating rules.

All other things being equal, a boat's maximum speed is determined by her waterline length. The maximum displacement speed of a boat in knots is approximately 1.4 times the square root of her waterline length in feet. Therefore the maximum theoretical speed of a 25 ft (7·5 m) displacement boat would be $1.4 \times \sqrt{25} = (1.4 \times 5) = 7$ knots. By the same calculation a boat of 36 ft (11 m) waterline length would have a maximum displacement speed of 8.4 knots.

Displacement speed refers to the speed of a boat which has to displace water as she moves forwards. This is limited by the wave which the displacement of water creates and over which the boat cannot climb. Planing hulls can achieve greater speeds because they lift out of the water and plane or skim on the surface.

The rating rules decree that a boat's handicap is based on her potential speed and, therefore, the longer the waterline length the higher her handicap. On the other hand beam is considered to be a speed reducing factor. So the bigger a boat in terms of width, the better her handicap. Yacht designers got to work on the very complicated handicap rating formula and came up with the concept of wider boats which gained a disproportionate drop in handicap compared with their drop in speed.

This has resulted in a very healthy design development leading to boats with greater beam and, therefore, more reserve buoyancy and so greater safety. The trend has spread from out-and-out racing yachts to cruiser racers and now family cruisers.

The extra beam brings many advantages to the cruising boat, the most obvious being more living space and comfort. More width enables the rig to be better supported, and the weight of ballast and the draft of the boat can be reduced because the hull has more inherent stability thanks to the increased buoyancy.

In some racing yachts, beam in the aft section is taken to such

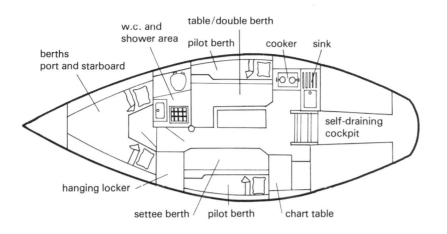

A typical modern broad-beamed cruising boat – only 29′ 6″ (9 m) long overall but with six berths: the Colvic Sailer.

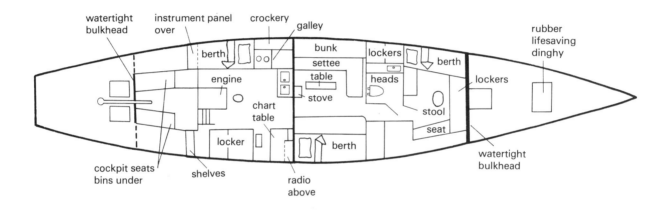

an extreme that the hull is virtually wedge shaped – very wide aft and very fine forward. Such boats will never sail themselves, but they have a high speed potential and good downwind performance. There are many good cruising boats which have this wedge shape too when looked at afloat and from above, while the underwater shape of the aft sections is reasonably fine and they retain some ability to sail themselves.

At the end of the day there is no argument that length means speed, and a long narrow boat will always outpace a short fat one given an equal driving force. Length is cheaper to build than beam, but a long narrow boat will have cramped 'corridor' accommodation, will heel over a lot, and will be a very wet boat to sail. Also, because she has little or no extra buoyancy when heeled, she will require a lot of ballast or a heavy keel and her righting movement will be slow.

A long narrow boat, 57′ (17 m) long overall but with only five berths – Gipsy Moth V now used as a charter yacht but originally built for speed.

Yachts built before, and for some time after, the war were nearly all of the long thin type. They had a tendency to 'submarine' through waves as water came up over the bows and back along the deck. Wet sailing was totally acceptable in the 1930s, but people do not expect it these days.

To sail well in a seaway, a boat needs to have some overhang beyond its waterline length to give her buoyancy fore and aft. The overhang at the bows should be fine enough to cut through the water and offer minimum resistance to the forward movement, at the same time providing sufficient buoyancy when the bows dip into the water. This is achieved by giving the bows a flare so that they retain their streamlined shape to cut through the water but provide increased buoyancy as they go deeper into the water.

The old fashioned long-keel, straight-stemmed boat which has good directional stability once underway at sea has no reserve buoyancy forward. In a heavy sea she just goes head first into waves instead of lifting over them, and if she starts pitching, the bows are driven deeper into the sea and will not lift until the foredeck is awash. A wet and most uncomfortable type of hull to sail in, and also very slow to respond to the helm.

While the bow section needs to be flared to go through the water, the aft section needs to be rounded to give maximum buoyancy lift and prevent waves from breaking over the stern and overwhelming the boat. At the same time a reasonably fine shape is required immediately below the rounded buoyancy to allow the sea to flow aft smoothly.

Overhang has the great advantage of increasing the actual waterline length of a boat when she is heeled over, which automatically increases her maximum displacement speed. This is fortunate because when a boat is well-heeled she loses some of the drive from her sails.

Theoretically, the longer the overhangs the longer the waterline length when heeled, and therefore the faster the boat could be sailed to windward. But there are practical limits. Too much overhang at each end would mean that when a boat started to pitch the extra weight at bow and stern would cause the hull to rock more violently—like two heavy people on a see-saw—and life aboard would be intolerable.

If you compare cruising yachts of twenty years ago with those built today you will note a remarkable increase in the height above water of the hulls and superstructure. It was once unlikely to find standing headroom anywhere on board a boat of less than 30ft (9·1 m) length. Today it is common in boats as small as 24ft (7·3 m), even if in only one small area.

This change in design, largely dictated by demand for more comfort afloat, has the disadvantage of greatly increasing the windage and, because the centre of gravity is raised, stability is reduced. However there is a compensating safety factor. At large angles of heel when the sidedeck is awash the increased height of the topsides (that part of a hull above the water) increases the boat's buoyancy – always provided that the coamings (sides) of the cockpit are sufficiently high to prevent water pouring in off the sidedeck. A boat with moderately high topsides, high sidedecks or flush decks is, in extreme sea conditions, far safer than a boat with low freeboard and a high coachroof (cabin top).

Quite different from the long or fin-keel configuration is the twin or bilge-keel boat which has two fin-type keels sticking out at angles either side of the hull like legs – and legs is what they are used as much of the time. These boats are immensely popular among those who sail in shoal waters and areas where harbours and moorings dry out at low tide. In some places they far outnumber the single keel boats.

The advantages are plain to see. A twin-keel boat can cross shallower water because twin keels are usually shorter than a single keel, and if she makes a mistake in negotiating a deep water channel and goes aground she will sit upright on her keels until the tide comes back again. Many owners and families use this facility to seek out shelving beaches and sandbanks on which to dry out between tides and use their boat as a mobile seaside chalet.

Having a smaller draft than equivalent size keel boats, they can more often be taken into shallow estuaries and creeks and up rivers to enjoy the scenery, and they can more easily find sheltered water when it is blowing out at sea. (see page 49)

There is a great amount of argument about the sailing performance of twin keel boats. The short answer is that there are no out-and-out racing boats with twin keels.

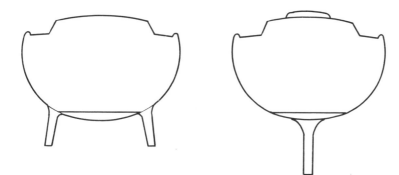

Twin keel and fin keel versions of the Colvic Sailer. These section drawings show the relatively shallow draft of the twin keel version.

The disadvantages are that the two keels combine to cause underwater turbulence and drag which slow down the hull's movement through the water; they suffer from more leeway than keel boats; and they are not as stable. Owners will claim that their boats are extremely stable, and they may be right. But stability is gained by keeping to a low rig or sail plan, and therefore they do not have as much driving power as they need. Many people do their cruising in light and moderate winds, and it is in just those conditions that a twin keel boat is relatively slow because she cannot get sufficient driving force from a light breeze.

Many classes of small cruising yachts are produced in the two versions, fin- and twin-keel. One or the other must be very much a design compromise, and it is most likely to be the twin keeler. Having said all that, they are still a very practical type of boat for coastal cruising, especially in shoal waters, provided no high performance is expected.

As more and more people have taken up yachting there is an ever-increasing number of owners who have overcome their initial limitations and are now looking for performance boats. The twin keel boat's performance will no longer satisfy them.

At the same time more and more boats are being built, but the existing ones are not falling apart or melting away so there is a continually increasing shortage of moorings. In the more popular areas marina berths are all taken and there are long waiting lists. Deep water moorings are congested and in many places cannot be increased or they would block the fairway.

This lack of space has made yacht designers think back to the 1920s and 1930s when small cabin sailers were left to fend for themselves up creeks and in mud berths or were hauled out onto dry land. Apart from the commercial and fishing harbours there were then few special facilities for yachts, and the smaller ones had to find whatever natural shelter and landing places they could.

Many small boats therefore had retractable keels which gave them good sailing ability when at sea and shoal draft advantages when they made a landfall. The trouble was that, being wooden boats, the hole in the hull to take the retractable keel was a weak point so they could be leaky and troublesome.

GRP (glass reinforced plastic – glassfibre) construction allows for a retractable keel housing to be provided as part of the hull moulding so that it is not only completely watertight but also acts as box-girder reinforcing. This has made the retractable keel boat feasible and there is a growing market for such boats, which have a far better performance than twin keelers and are truly shoal draft when their keels are retracted. They can be moored where other boats cannot go and, in smaller sizes, are easy to trail.

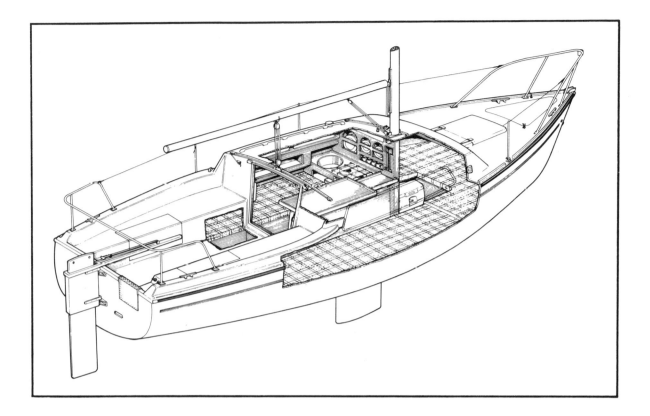

Trailability is a most noticeable trend recently, and is likely to continue as berths and moorings become harder to find and more expensive. A 20ft (6m) sailing cruiser can be moved quickly across country on the motorways by a reasonable-sized car, making it possible to visit a variety of sailing areas in any one season.

The initial cost of a trailer and the higher petrol consumption when trailing still do not add up to the cost of keeping a boat in a marina in a fashionable sailing centre. A boat of about 20ft (6m) does not allow for luxury living on board – the accommodation provides for a way of life somewhere between camping and caravanning – but the compensation is a performance boat which does not cost money when it is not being used.

The small retractable keel boat is likely to be of light displacement and have the performance of an over-sized dinghy. In sheltered waters or in light winds she will be delightfully easy to sail and very responsive, but in the open sea in strong winds she might be a little hair raising for the beginner because she will be fast and need a lot of skill to control.

Timpenny 670, a popular and typical trailer sailer, designed in Australia with retractable keel and rudder, and high performance. The overall length is 22ft (6.62m).

43

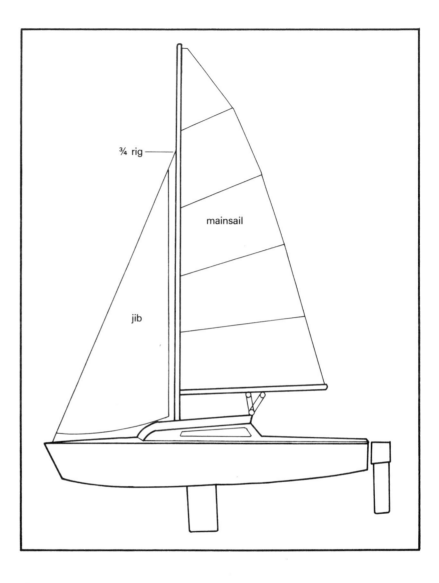

¾ rig

mainsail

jib

A fractional rig.

THE RIG

The bermudan sloop with one mast, a mainsail and one headsail—in this instance called a jib—is far and away the most common rig afloat today. Normally this is a masthead rig, so called because both the mainsail and the jib go right to the top of the mast.

On small and medium-sized boats it is a most efficient and easily-handled rig. When turning to windward (tacking) there is only one sail, the jib, to be handled. But on big boats the height of the mast and the size of the sails, especially the jib, can be so great that they are difficult to handle when sail has to be

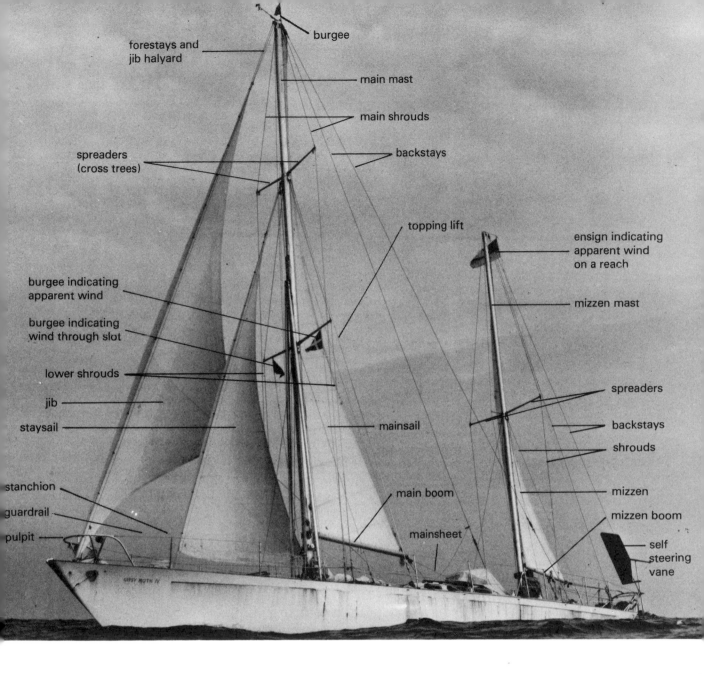

forestays and
jib halyard

burgee

main mast

main shrouds

spreaders
(cross trees)

backstays

topping lift

ensign indicating
apparent wind
on a reach

burgee indicating
apparent wind

burgee indicating
wind through slot

mizzen mast

lower shrouds

jib

staysail

mainsail

spreaders

backstays

shrouds

stanchion

guardrail

pulpit

main boom

mainsheet

mizzen

mizzen boom

self
steering
vane

A famous staysail ketch,
Gipsy Moth IV.

reduced or changed in heavy weather. Ocean racers of 40–50 ft
(12·5–15 m) still have this rig, but they carry large, strong and
highly trained crews.

An alternative to the masthead sloop is the seven-eighth or
three-quarter rig; there are variations depending on the actual
distance between the top of the forestay and the top of the mast.
Mast compression forces are reduced because the standing rigging
is attached lower down, so the top part of the mast can be narrower
and lighter allowing it to flex and impart a better shape to the
mainsail. This facility can compensate for the shorter luff on the
headsail, which would otherwise impair windward performance.

burgee indicating
apparent wind

burgee indicating
wind through slot

leeward
jib sheet

weather
jib sheet

A staysail ketch, *Gipsy Moth IV*
again.

For very large cruising boats the cutter rig is more practical. This is very similar to the sloop, but the mast is stepped a little further aft and two headsails are set. One is the jib on the forestay and the other, the staysail, is set on an inner stay running from about three-quarters the way up the mast to a point on the deck between the foot of the mast and the bows.

Very often the tack of the jib is at the end of a bowsprit, and the staysail tack is then attached at the bows. Although the total sail area may be larger on a cutter than a sloop of the same size, the three sails individually are smaller and therefore easier to handle. It is in strong winds that this type of rig scores because with two headsails there are two slots to accelerate the flow of air. In light winds the staysail can be lowered and a very large headsail set with its leech coming well aft of the mast so transforming a cutter to a sloop rig.

The ketch and the yawl are two-masted rigs. The mainmast

carries a sloop rig and the much shorter mast near the stern carries a mizzen sail. If the mizzenmast is behind the rudder post the boat is a yawl; if it is in front of the rudder post she is a ketch.

Because it is difficult, or impossible, to fully stay a mast right on the stern of a boat, a yawl has a smaller mizzen mast and sail and a larger mainsail than a ketch, which can have quite a big mizzen and somewhat smaller main. They are convenient rigs for a cruising boat because the mainsail can be lowered in heavy winds and the boat sailed with just the mizzen and jib.

A mizzen staysail can also be set between the two masts for extra drive. The mizzen is a particularly helpful sail on a reach, but when beating to windward it is hit by wind deflected off the mainsail and has to be set much flatter than the main. It then does little more than increase the angle of heel. On a dead run it tends to cause eddies which increase the chances of the main gybing.

Two large ocean racing yachts close hauled on the starboard and port tacks. The true wind is blowing directly towards the camera. The boat in the foreground, with her mizzen mast aft of the rudder, is a yawl. The other yacht is a sloop.

A small junk rigged cruising boat and a rather old fashioned ketch rigged motor sailer.

Opposite above When the tide goes out the twin keel boat becomes a seaside chalet. *Opposite below* One of the joys of cruising is making landfalls in remote unspoilt places.

Some owners can achieve marvels of self-steering by balancing the sails and using the mizzen as a wind rudder. A mizzen set when the boat is at anchor will help her to lie head to wind. When going under engine alone the mizzen makes an excellent steadying sail to reduce rolling–in fact many motor boats and fishing boats carry a mizzen for that very purpose.

The schooner has two masts of equal size, or else a mainmast with a slightly smaller foremast. This rig allows a number of sails to be set, for example a flying jib set on a bowsprit, a jib, a staysail, a foresail and a main. Each of these sails steadies and directs the air flow onto the next one behind it. But if they are not well trimmed they will blanket each other and performance will be poor.

If properly understood it is a safe and manageable rig for bigger cruising boats of 40 ft (12·5 m) and over because it provides an enormous area of driving sail broken down into relatively small sections. It is not the ideal rig for close winded sailing or a dead run, but can be very fast on a reach.

The schooner has always been more popular in North America than in European waters; it is a big ship rig and is more suited to long downwind and trade wind passages. Large schooners are not for afternoon sailing in confined and crowded waters, and those who have schooners need the time in which to make long cruises offshore to gain the advantage of this essentially ocean-going rig.

The Chinese junk rig would have been considered a joke among yachtsmen in the northern hemisphere a generation ago, but it has now become a standard rig for a few modern yachts. In essence the sail or sails of a junk rig are similar to the old European square sails in that they are hoisted on a yard, but they are battened right across their width at intervals from head to foot. In theory such a sail should work almost as effectively as an aeroplane wing and enable a boat to sail extremely close to the wind. The control of these sails is very complicated to look at but simple to operate.

The trim of each sail is controlled by a spider's web of little sheets attached to the outer ends of each sail batten and they all lead via bridles and friction blocks to one main sheet. This rig can be operated single-handed from the cockpit and when the time comes to shorten sail they can be wholly or partly folded up or down like a lady's fan.

You are unlikely to meet with the junk rig when you start sailing, but if you do the owner will almost certainly be an out-and-out buff cast in the same mould as the old gaffer or steam boat owner. From him you will learn how this Chinese puzzle works better than from any book.

The old square rig is now preserved on the great sail training ships and a few smaller types such as the brigantine which is part square and part schooner rigged. However, many a long-distance cruising skipper carries a square sail in his wardrobe of sails which he hoists for long downwind passages. A yacht setting off to make a trade wind run across the Atlantic or any other ocean should make good use of such a sail.

BUILDING MATERIALS

The materials of which a boat is made are not always apparent at a distance or from a casual glance, and they do not make any difference to the way a boat is sailed. Seamanship calls for the same skills, concentration and discipline whatever the boat. But what it is made of is of very great importance when it comes to the boat in which you plan to invest your money and which you will have to look after.

Wood is the most attractive of all boat building materials, but is now a luxury beyond the reach of all but the richest owners. Not only is well seasoned timber difficult to come by and expensive to buy, but the craftsmen shipwrights who can build wooden yachts are a dying race. Where they can be found their labour is expensive because it is intensive.

Close hauled into a midsummer sunset on the last tack of the day making for a quiet anchorage.

Wooden boat building does not lend itself to mass production or even series production. Where it does come into its own, when money is no object, is in the building of a one-off boat to an owner's individual requirements. A wooden boat is somewhat like a piece of sculpture; it is unique, no two are exactly the same.

The major drawback to wooden boats is that they require constant maintenance. Other materials can be allowed to get dirty, scratched and shabby and they will remain in one piece and watertight. Once wood is neglected it will start to rot. Even so, if a man wants to buy a boat to last him his lifetime and is prepared to look after her, a well-built wooden boat would – despite the enormously high initial cost – be an excellent investment.

But we live in an age of continuous development, part exchange, trading up, and built-in obsolescence – even in boats. Few people now want a lifetime love affair with one boat. Boats like houses, cars and electronic gadgetry are an outward sign of rising affluence or credit rating coupled, in many cases, with a most understandable desire to take advantage of the ever-changing advances in technology. Yesterday's boat may be loved today, but she will be callously traded in for something better tomorrow.

This state of affairs was brought about by the development of GRP which enables hulls, decks and other parts to be built in moulds on a series production basis. They are now built in factories rather than in boatyards.

Glassfibre boats, as they are termed, were unknown 25 years ago, and when they first appeared people laughed and said they were a seven-day wonder, that they would soon fall to pieces, and who wanted a plastic boat anyway. The initial, but somewhat bogus, claim that GRP required no maintenance was a strong selling point, and volume sales enabled the industry to improve its materials and moulding techniques until today it is a totally acceptable building material for the finest boats.

It has a high strength-to-weight ratio, it allows for shapes to be moulded which in any other material would be impossible to achieve, and a whole hull can be produced without any joins and therefore be completely watertight. The internal furniture and compartments are often in the form of one-piece mouldings bonded to the hull moulding, so that the whole becomes an immensely strong box-girder structure.

It is an extremely practical form of building, but it does mean that the owner can make no alterations to the interior layout afterwards, nor can he ask for modifications during the building stage. Only curtains and cushions will distinguish his boat from every other one out of the same mould.

The GRP hull requires little maintenance compared with a

wooden one, but the bottom does need to be painted every year with anti-fouling because plastic is not immune to marine growths, and a dirty hull makes a slow boat.

A GRP hull has great tensile strength and will flex and return to its proper shape when it receives a moderate knock, but it has less resistance to damage from sharp objects than wood or steel. It is watertight because it has an outer gel coat of pure resin, but if that gel coat is scored through, water will penetrate into the glass fibres and cause delamination. It is therefore necessary after a period to paint the hull to keep it watertight.

Steel is very much the material for large one-off boats which are going to sail round the world and must stand up to heavy punishment. Constant maintenance is required as rust must not be allowed to develop, and that means frequent painting. Steel can be easily and rapidly corroded away by electrolysis, so electrical installations must be professionally done and the hull protected by strategically placed sacrificial anodes. There may also be problems with the compass, which will need regular expert adjusting.

Aluminium alloys have now been developed with a high resistance to sea water and electrolysis, and a weight saving between alloys and steel of between 30 per cent and 50 per cent can be achieved. But alloy construction is a very specialised business, and repair yards that understand the problems and are equipped to do alloy welding are few and far between.

Ferro cement boat building now has a vogue among amateur builders because it appears to be reasonably cheap and not too demanding in skill. A wire mesh sheath is stretched over a framework of steel rods bent to the shape of the hull and welded together, and is then 'plastered' over with cement. The final application of the cement calls for the skills of a professional plasterer, and also a large labour force for a short period because it all has to be applied in one 'go'. The advantages are that it wears well, is resistant to shock, and can be formed in almost any shape.

An excellent but still expensive form of wood construction is cold or hot moulding. A wooden frame is built over which thin strips of wood, little thicker than veneer, are laid in criss-cross layers. In cold moulding each layer is glued and stapled and the glue is allowed to set naturally before the next layer is put on. In hot moulding pressure and heat are used.

With either method a very strong, light and watertight hull is produced, and the glues form a perfect protection against wood borers like gribble and toredo, which are the great menace of wooden boats. With this type of construction the ribs and stringers are usually laminated instead of being made from solid wood, which increases the hull strength while keeping the weight down.

4. Before you go sailing

When you first go sailing the other crew members may be strangers to you, perhaps even strangers to each other. Even if you have met them before, or if they are all personal friends, they are likely to adopt somewhat different attitudes and behaviour on a boat to those they normally exhibit ashore. This will be particularly noticeable if they are experienced sailors and you are on your first cruise.

For any sailing to be successful and enjoyable the crew must become good mates from the very start. The success and possibly the safety of even the shortest cruise will depend on everyone working together and being able to live together in a confined space. In the beginning you will be judged by your behaviour, not by your lack of seamanship.

Seamanlike behaviour, because it is so much commonsense, is easier to learn and practise than seamanship. It starts at home with your own preparations, particularly deciding what to take with you and what to leave behind. You are not going on holiday with a car which can be loaded with luggage, nor will you be living in an hotel room with cupboards, wardrobe and bath and plenty of shops a few floors down.

You are going to stay on board someone else's miniature floating home in which storage space, by domestic standards, will be ridiculously small and awkwardly shaped. There is not likely to be room for more than bare essentials, but you will be expected to arrive equipped for a very exposed life in good and bad weather.

Boats have curved sides and therefore curved storage spaces, so you will not have the convenience of living out of a suitcase; if you take one you will almost certainly be asked to leave it ashore. Kit bags, duffle bags and holdalls which can be stuffed into odd-shaped spaces are the only permissible luggage on a boat. If you are lucky there may be space to hang one jacket and a pair of trousers, but they are likely to get very crushed.

It is as well to be prepared for the odd yacht club that insists on jackets and ties in the dining room as do some restaurants, and it does everybody's morale a lot of good if ladies on board can make the transformation from T-shirts and jeans to a skirt and top when they go ashore. Otherwise there is no room or reason for smart clothes on a boat.

If you are fortunate enough to be going sailing in a semi-tropical or Mediterranean climate the question of clothing is almost irrelevant—you hardly need any. But there is one hazard to guard against. The strength of the sun's rays is almost doubled by being reflected off the sea, but because of the cooling effect of the apparent wind when sailing you will not feel its full heat. It is easy to become badly sunburned without realising what is happening until it is too late. Shoulders, forearms and thighs are the most vulnerable parts, and white or pink bodies should wear trousers and long sleeves at least during the middle of the day. If you get sunburned it will not only be very painful, but you will have to stay in the shade for a couple of days and be unable to take part in the sailing, so you are bound to be a bit of a nuisance to the rest of the crew who will have to look after you and do your work.

In northern latitudes warm clothing is very important because even in the middle of a good summer the weather can deteriorate and become very cold at sea, especially at night. It is always much cooler on a boat than on the land because there is no shelter from the wind or spray, so do not be misled by warm weather at home or the weather forecasts for inland.

Two or three sweaters of varying weights are essential—a light one to put on at the first sign of getting chilly and before you start losing body heat, and a heavier one for when it is really cold. Trapped air is the finest form of insulation, so several layers of lightweight clothing are better than one enormously thick sweater. Wool is by far the best material, being far warmer than synthetic fibres even when wet.

Sitting still in the cockpit or on deck in a breeze can be very chilling, and working on deck going to windward is often very wet. Wind chill increases rapidly when you are wet; and tiredness, often unavoidable on a long passage, also reduces the body temperature. Thermal underwear is very comforting when sailing early or late in the season and for night passages, and it does not make a lot of bulk.

It is very difficult to dry clothes on a boat unless they can be laid out on deck in hot sun. Even then, if they have been soaked in sea water the salt crystals imbedded in them are hydroscopic and as soon as the humidity rises they will become damp again. They will not remain dry until after they have been rinsed in

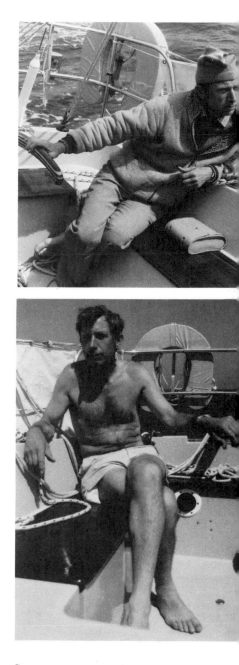

Same man, same cruise, same time on different days. *Above* Sailing to windward in a good breeze, it is chilly in the cockpit. *Below* When there is plenty of sun and no wind, the cockpit is a sun trap.

fresh water, which is unlikely to be possible on a boat with its limited water supply. So for any trip longer than a day it is most advisable to take a change of dry clothing.

The number of times you will want to change into clean fresh clothes during a longer cruise will depend on your own fastidiousness. Unless work has to be done on the engine, you do not get really dirty on a boat but you do get sweaty and smelly.

A limited water supply and the awkwardness of miniature wash basins, particularly on a heeling boat, make it tempting to go unwashed and unshaven for two or three days at a time. In rough weather it can take a lot of self-discipline and determined effort to shut yourself up in a claustrophobic closet in the forward part of a rolling or pitching boat, strip off, and wash down in a few pints of tepid water.

But the rejuvenation which follows, and the sensual satisfaction of putting on sweet-smelling, crisp, clean underwear and shirt does wonders for the morale. It can banish boredom, tiredness and even apprehension.

The job is made easier if you have done your packing properly. Clothing is more likely to be sweet-smelling, crisp and clean if it has been packed in plastic bags so that it does not come into contact with damp locker walls or soak up drips from condensation. Transparent bags enable you to rummage for what you want without having to tip everything out all over the cabin.

Spare plastic bags are also the best way to stow the stale clothing you have discarded. It is very difficult to have a stand-up wash if you have forgotten to bring a flannel or sponge, and you will have a messy problem unless your soap dish has a tight lid. Towels get very wet and are difficult to dry except on those days when they can be set flying from the rigging. It is better to take two or three small towels than one big one which will always be damp when you want to use it.

In fine weather with gentle winds a lightweight canvas or heavy cotton sailing smock or an anorak is sufficient windbreak for sitting in the cockpit, working on deck and going ashore. But when the wind gets up and it is wet on board, light waterproofs as sold for camping and walking are not really good enough.

You need oilskins—oilies, as they are commonly called. Oilskins is really an old fashioned word which does not properly describe modern waterproof sailing gear. If you first go sailing on a school or charter boat you will almost certainly be told that oilies are supplied or can be hired. Should you have any reason to doubt your continued interest in sailing, for the first time it would be wise to wear what is provided and you will save yourself a lot of money.

Close hauled in a strong breeze is when you need your oilies.

Good oilies are expensive, and cheap ones are useless; they will not fit comfortably, they will probably leak at the seams, and tear the first time they catch on something. Even a small tear acts as a drain hole for water running down the fabric which will soon soak a large area of clothing underneath. When you stop working wet clothes are very cold.

Good oilies are designed with adequate ventilation to prevent internal condensation. The material is tough enough to withstand a lot of wear and tear on a boat, and the knees and backsides are reinforced. Jacket fastenings are large, non-jamming, rustproof zip fasteners with buttoning or Velcro fastening flaps over them. Pockets have double flaps so that they too are waterproof, and cuffs and trouser bottoms have adjustable fastenings.

Water always finds its way down collars, so take a supply of towelling scarves to wear round your neck to form a watertight gasket. An attached oilskin hood keeps water off the back of the neck and head, but it also tends to make you deaf. The traditional sou'wester takes a lot of beating. With its big brim at

Prepared for the worst—safety harness, good oilies, towelling scarf and wooly hat.

the back to protect the neck, and one on the front to stop water running down into your eyes, it is the nearest thing to a nautical umbrella, and it leaves your ears open to hear orders.

Despite the expense, if you are serious about your sailing and have the firm intent to keep it up you might as well start off with good waterproof gear. You will be faced with a wide variety of makes and styles, but you are unlikely to make a mistake if you choose a brand which is used by ocean racing crews; a product which can stand up to that toughest of all sailing will certainly be good enough for your needs. Lightweight dinghy sailing gear is also useful as a second outfit, if you can afford it, to keep the spray off on warm days, but it will not keep you warm and dry in heavy weather.

The most practical outfit is a two-piece suit with the trousers held up by braces and rising well up the chest. One-piece suits, which may be marginally more waterproof in very bad conditions, are awkward to put on and take off in a cabin and cause uncomfortable delay when nature calls!

Wet hands can get very cold, so a pair of woollen gloves are a great comfort. There are special sailing gloves, and they are certainly a practical proposition for women when it comes to rope work.

Approximately 18 per cent of body heat is lost through the head, so a woollen hat is more than a decoration. A friend of mine, a skipper with a lifetime's experience, always wears a cloth cap. Being flat it does not blow off or get caught in rigging, and the peak acts as a sunshade when taking bearings or keeping a lookout.

Most people wear jeans all the time on board, but early and late in the season an old pair of heavier-weight trousers are a warmer bet. Beware of flared bottoms though which can catch on deck fittings.

Conditions for a safety harness, but its line should not be clipped to the guardrail. If he goes overboard from a boat going at speed in these conditions he will be swept aft, and the lifeline shackle will be whipped back and pulled up hard against the next stanchion which could be broken off or pulled out of its deck mounting.

Last, but not least, footwear. In fine weather you need deck shoes. They can be gym shoes, tennis shoes or proper yachting deck shoes, but they must have soles which are guaranteed not to slip on wet surfaces and they must not be black rubber which leaves marks.

When it is at all wet, rubber boots designed for deck work—not for gardening, fishing or farmwork—are as important as oilies. On a wet deck, canvas or denim shoes will soon get soaked, and so will socks and trouser ends. There are short ankle boots and calf length ones. The latter, although heavier and bulkier to carry and stow, are more useful.

Rubber boots are cold, so should be large enough to take fairly thick socks. Boots are worn inside, not over, the trouser legs of your oilies so that water does not drain down into them.

Pack several pairs of socks. Whatever precautions you take, you are bound to have wet feet, possibly for hours at a time, and wet feet inside rubber boots are a fertile breeding ground for the fungus which produces athlete's foot. Dry your feet as often as you can and treat them to dry socks and shoes. If you use boots when it is wet your deck shoes will remain dry.

There are two other essential items of sailing gear which must be available for every crew member—a lifejacket and safety

Children should wear a safety harness on deck when the boat is underway, even in harbour. On a mooring or at anchor with no tide running a life jacket is a less restricting alternative. Note the safety line is shackled to a fixed point on the pulpit.

harness. More often than not both are provided by the owner of the boat, especially the latter which is simply a webbing harness with snap shackles. Since it is completely adjustable there is nothing to be gained by taking your own personal one. But make sure that you adjust your safety harness to fit before you have to put it on on a dark rough night.

Although on most cruising boats safety harnesses are worn more often than lifejackets, a lifejacket is more personal and should be comfortable to wear and work in and, above all, it should be one which you know how to put on in a hurry. All lifejackets and safety equipment must be to an approved standard (BSI in Britain).

Lifejackets supplied on school boats, while being of an approved type and adequate for their purpose, may be one of the less expensive designs and therefore a bit bulky or awkward to wear when working. There is much to be said for owning your own lifejacket, looking after it, and knowing that it will work when you need it.

If you are prepared to put your money where your enthusiasm is you can go afloat fully and independently equipped all in one piece with the ultimate in sailing gear—the ocean racing-type waterproof suit with its own built-in safety harness and inflatable lifejacket. It is lined inside for comfort and has a very efficient ventilation arrangement. With a pair of seaboots on, the hood up, and warm clothes underneath you will be snug and dry in the very worst conditions and fully equipped for personal safety.

After sorting out your clothes—old sweaters and frayed shirts can have a new lease of life at sea—consider very carefully what personal items you will need. High on the list should be seasick pills; none of us is immune, and prevention is better than cure. Start on a course the night before sailing and continue on it until you are sure you have found your sea legs. It would be wise to have a word with your doctor in the first instance.

Leave behind anything which is valuable or which could rust or corrode in salt air, let alone sea water. Leather can be ruined by salt water, and so can a good watch; take either a waterproof one or a cheap one. Cameras with built-in light-meters and other electronic components in them will require a major and expensive servicing if they get the minutest drop of sea water on them. You take a good camera to sea at your peril.

Check up on whether you need to take your own sleeping bag and pillow, and if you are expected to contribute to the food stores in cash or in kind. Sailing schools and charterers will normally send you a check list of essential items to take with you.

When it comes to drink it is always wrong, except on a known dry boat, to arrive empty handed. But a bottle of sherry will not be considered much of a contribution by a beer-drinking crew.

Heavy smokers may have problems. There are skippers who do not allow smoking anywhere on board; others allow it only in the cockpit or on deck. Tobacco smoke in the small confines of a cabin can be revolting to non-smokers. If you are a heavy smoker you may have to modify your habit. It is not so bad when the boat is underway because there will be a good through-draught, but in harbour if you smoke down below choose a place to sit which is down wind of the non-smokers.

Lighters are better than matches, which easily become damp and useless. Non-safety matches are a menace on glassfibre boats; if one is dropped and then trodden on, the head will flare up, melt the gel coat, and leave an irremovable burn mark.

When you have sorted out everything that you want to take you should be able to carry it all in one go yourself. If you need a hand to help carry your gear you are probably taking too much, unless you are going for an extended cruise on a large yacht.

The old adage that time and tide wait for no man is very true, so it is important to arrive well on time when you have a date to go sailing. If the skipper has to miss a tide because you are late it may mean sailing is delayed for eight hours or more.

It is equally true that man very often has to wait for wind and tide, so you must be philosophical if sailing is delayed for either reason or because of an adverse weather forecast. This is often a cause of frustration to people who have booked a sailing course or are paying a charter fee for a boat and find themselves stuck in harbour for a day.

But it does have some advantages for the novice. A great deal of practical instruction can be given on a stationary boat, and it gives a strange crew time to get to know each other and the boat.

Never try to persuade a skipper to sail against his better judgement; it will only upset the relationship and, in the unlikely event of his yielding, you will probably have a more miserable time than you bargained for. The skipper of a boat is responsible for every decision made and order given. He is in command every bit as much as is the captain of a large ship.

A boat cannot be sailed by committee or by argument. Whatever your ideas about democracy and equality, leave them ashore when you go sailing. If you cannot stomach this old fashioned concept of authority, and the discipline which it imposes, you will not be able to enjoy sailing.

Also, unless and until you have learnt to take orders, even in the context of sailing for pleasure, you will not be competent to command a crew of your own. There has to be respect on both sides if skipper and crew are to work efficiently and happily together. There are far too many wives and children who come to hate sailing because the husband never learned that lesson.

5. Going on board

If the boat is alongside a pontoon in a marina going on board presents no problems, but remember not to wear hard-soled shoes or high heels, or to take mud and dirt onto clean decks.

When you have to climb down a ladder against a harbour wall to get on board do not put your feet on a stanchion or the guard-rail – they were not designed to take your weight at that angle. Go down low enough on the ladder to get a firm footing on the deck before taking your hands off the ladder, and try not to get your legs crossed in the process. If you step onto the edge of the boat outside the guardrail there is the risk of slipping down between boat and harbour wall, or of getting a foot crushed if the boat should surge from the wash of a passing boat.

You may have to climb over the decks of other boats to get to your own. Make your way via their foredecks, not across their cockpits or aft decks which is considered an intrusion of privacy and bad form.

The only safe way to go down a ladder is to use both hands. Gear should be handed down not carried down, unless it can be slung on the back as in the case of a rucksack. Very painful accidents have happened to people trying to go down a ladder carrying gear in one hand and holding on with the other. The weight of the gear tends to swing the body to one side, and if one foot should slip as the other is between rungs you would be left hanging by one arm. You are then likely to loose your grip and fall.

Going out to a boat on a mooring or at anchor in a small tender may look a simple operation, and if it is only a short row across flat still water it may be so. However, it is a fact that more people are drowned every year on their way to and from boat and shore than are drowned falling overboard at sea.

The use of small yacht tenders calls for its own form of seamanship. More often than not they are stowed on the coachroof or, if inflatables, they are deflated and rolled up on deck or put in a locker. They are therefore, of necessity, rather small—sometimes too small to be stable when loaded with a crew and their gear.

When a tender is overloaded it sits low in the water with very little freeboard as all its reserve buoyancy is being used to support the extra weight. In that state it is very sluggish and does not lift to waves or swell. In a chop—and it can be very choppy when the wind is blowing against the tide—or when meeting the wash of a passing boat, water will slop in. This only has to happen a few times on a trip and a tender can become waterlogged. A tender without any built-in buoyancy will then sink. If it does have sufficient built-in buoyancy or is an inflatable it will not sink, but it will then take very little movement from the water or from those on board to capsize it.

Such accidents are not too serious in water shallow enough to wade ashore in or in still water provided everyone is a strong swimmer or is wearing a lifejacket. The biggest danger is being swept seawards on an out-going tide, especially at night when no one can see you.

Your lifejacket will prevent you from drowning, but what about exposure? In the North Sea, for example, the mean temperature rarely rises above 50°F (10°C) for nine months of the year, which gives a healthy adult a maximum survival time of only two hours before hypothermia becomes fatal. That time is very much reduced if the victim has alcohol in his blood. A sobering thought after a good night ashore. It therefore behoves everyone to take this activity seriously and never to fool around in small boats.

Should you be unfortunate enough to fall in the water with no immediate hope of being rescued, get into the floating position supported by your lifejacket and lie still. Unlike on the land where one keeps moving to stay warm, in the water movement must be kept to the absolute minimum. The reason is that the water in your clothes next to your skin will be warmed by your body heat, and as long as it is not disturbed will give you some protection from the cold. But movement will circulate cold water through your clothes which will wash away the layer of warm water and then your body will loose heat rapidly.

The first rule is not to overload a tender, but to make more trips with fewer people or less gear on board. But human nature being what it is impatience too often over-rules prudence.

When other people are already in the tender choose a place for yourself which will keep the weight as evenly distributed as possible. Do not let go of your hand-hold ashore until you have got both feet firmly in position, and then sit down immediately and keep still. If you have to change places do not stand up; do it in the sitting position. Do not rock the boat.

In a rigid tender sit on one of the thwarts (cross benches),

Small children must never, never be allowed in a tender without wearing lifejackets or buoyancy aids. Mother could have set a better example, but it is obviously a very calm day and, hopefully, there is no tide running.

Left Never stand on the side of a rigid tender or hang onto the flexible guardrail.
Right The clumsy approach with a tender. If it drifts backwards he could end up in the water.

never on the side. Any marked uneven distribution of weight will make the boat unstable and difficult to row, and also difficult to steer either with oars or an outboard motor.

If an outboard-driven tender is loaded stern down the efficiency of the propeller will be considerably reduced and dirty water from it will probably slop into the boat. Worse, any sudden slowing down will bring two or three gallons of water from its wake pouring in over the stern.

Never be shy about wearing a lifejacket when you have to make a trip in a small tender with the wind blowing, a tide running, or the water at all choppy. It is on such occasions—which can occur any day on a cruise—that a waterproof sailing jacket with its own built-in or inflatable buoyancy is so useful. It protects against the wind and spray, it looks right, and it gets rid of the problem of what to do with a separate lifejacket while you are ashore.

Tenders more often than not have some water in them, and underway this will slosh about and soak anything that is lying in the bottom—including your feet. The best way to carry your sailing boots out to the boat is on your feet otherwise you will most likely arrive on board with wet shoes, socks and trouser legs. If the tender is leaving from a slipway there is a fair chance that you will have to paddle to get into it, which is no problem with boots on.

Never step on the side of a small tender. It will tip up and, at the same time, be pushed away from you. At the best it will ship water; at the worst you will end up in the drink. It is possible to step onto the sponson (side) of an inflatable dinghy without it tipping, but only if it is securely tied alongside or being held in position, otherwise you will send it sliding away from you.

Should an unexpected dollop of cold water hit your backside do not jump up in consternation—it is one way to upset a loaded boat. In fact, in a loaded boat with little freeboard you must sit perfectly still throughout the trip. If conditions are likely to be at all wet the wise man will slip into his waterproof trousers as well as wear his sea boots.

When coming alongside the yacht make sure that you are not holding onto the side of the tender with your fingers over the edge; they make poor and painful fenders.

6. Settling in and sorting out

There are many ways of scrambling on board a boat from a tender, but only one correct way and that depends on the tender being secured alongside the boat level with the shrouds. When your turn comes to go on board stand with your feet as near the centre of the tender as possible – in a rigid tender you can stand on the centre thwart, in an inflatable it can be the sponson – and take hold of a shroud in each hand.

Keep the tender in to the side of the boat with one foot while you lift the other to step onto the sidedeck, taking your weight on your arms. Heave yourself up between the shrouds and bring your second foot up onto the sidedeck without pushing down on the tender.

Once you have both feet on the edge of the deck, climb over the guardrail keeping your balance with your hands on the shrouds. Never grab the wire guardrail or safety line between the stanchions. It is too thin to be a good handhold and, being flexible, will bow out under your weight so that you will end up hanging out over the water instead of leaning into the boat. A most awkward position. Some skippers provide a boarding ladder or steps on the side or stern of the boat. Obviously they do make life easier.

When safely on board, offer to take any gear which is ready to be handed up from the tender, and carry it aft into the cockpit. Do not leave anything lying on the side deck from where it can so easily roll or be knocked into the water, and where it obstructs the already narrow walkway.

Once everyone and everything has been transferred on board the boat will probably look chaotic littered with personal baggage, boxes of food and drink, possibly a sailbag or two and other boat gear as well as cans of fuel and water. This is the moment when the stranger to the boat feels most inadequate. There is obviously so much to do, but he does not know the form. What is he supposed to do? What jobs does the skipper want done first? Where does everything go?

The right approach with the tender alongside. *Above* Secure the painter before standing up . . . *Below* then hold onto the shrouds and step onto the side deck with one foot, using the other foot to steady the tender alongside.

65

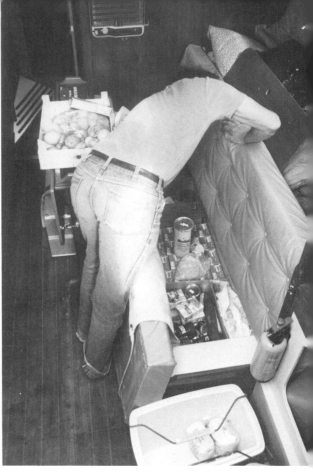

Above left Chaos in the cockpit before stowing begins.
Above right A place for everything, and the bilge locker under the bunks in the saloon is the place for bulk stores that are not in constant demand . . . . .
Below otherwise off-watch crew will have their rest disturbed. The lower berth is also a settee, and is a large item to open up when the boat is heeling or pitching. The two crew are taking a nap; it is a golden rule when making long passages which include night sailing that everybody gets some sleep during the day.

Opposite Resting in the noon day heat among the Greek Islands – one of the pleasures of flotilla sailing.

On a boat more than anywhere else there must be a place for everything and everything must be in its place, otherwise there is chaos. Never put anything away unless you are sure that it is the right place. On a school boat the skipper will almost certainly give everybody a job and show them how to do it as part of their instruction.

If there is a gas cooker the first person to go below would do well to bend down and have a good sniff in case the gas has been leaking. Butane gas is heavier than air, and if there has been a leak it will be lying in the bottom of the boat. Should anybody strike a match, or should there be a spark from the boat's electrical equipment, it may be your last moment on the boat if not this earth.

If gas is lying in the bottom (bilges) the skipper will have to take up the floorboards to clear it. Sometimes the bilge pump is used to extract the gas, and people have been known to ladle it out with saucepans!

The electrical system should have a battery isolation switch to prevent any drain from unsuspected voltage leaks or shorts in the system while the boat is shut down. Before any lights or other electrical equipment can be used–such as the boat's radio to listen to a forecast–the isolation switch must be turned on. The stranger to a boat would do well at this juncture to familiarise himself with the positions and functions of the boat's domestic switches.

At night time be sparing with the lights; do not switch them on unnecessarily. Electricity at home is taken for granted, and lighting costs very little. On a boat all electricity has to be stored in batteries which have to be charged by running the engine. An expensive and irritatingly noisy business if the engine is not being used to drive the boat at the same time.

Think of what happens if a car is left parked with its headlights on. After perhaps only an hour the battery is too flat to start the engine. The same applies if too many lights are used for any length of time on a boat. Even though it is a sailing boat the auxiliary engine is not just a convenience; it is an important item of safety equipment, but only if it will start instantly when required. Navigation lights and the radio are also essential to safety and need battery power. Many boats have two batteries–one for lighting and one for engine starting. It is important that the change-over switch is always in the right position.

A boat which has been left unoccupied for several days can be full of stale air and smell musty, and may be damp and clammy with condensation. If it is not pouring with rain, it is a good idea to open the hatches straight away to air the boat.

Before anyone can relax the personal gear and boat stores

Drifting slowly before the wind with sails goosewinged.

Left The galley layout in a 30ft (9m) yacht. The gas stove is gimballed so that it can be used when the boat is heeled. The companionway steps on the left are hinged so that they swing sideways to give access to the engine compartment.
Right The heads on a 30ft (9m) cruising yacht. The panel in the floor has to be lifted to get at the inlet and outlet seacocks before and after use when sailing.

lying on the deck and in the cockpit must be stowed. Sail bags are normally kept in lockers in the cockpit or up forward. The skipper will know what storage space is available for food, boat gear and personal belongings and he will have his own stowage plan. It is essential to conform to this otherwise there will be confusion.

Items which are in constant demand or need frequent replenishment will be stowed in the most accessible places, whereas reserves and little-used stores can be stowed under bunks or in the bilges. It should never be necessary to get someone out of his bunk in the middle of the night to get a carton of milk or to get yourself an extra sweater.

You will be given your own bit of stowage space and your own bunk. Put things which you will need frequently or in a hurry in the most easily-reached place, and stow the rest out of the way.

If you are going to sail at night your bunk may be used by other crew members when you are on watch, so it is not a permanent dump for your gear. If it is in the forecabin it may be needed for temporary sail stowage while sailing; if it is in the saloon it is also a public seat. Anyway, when a boat heels, gear left on a bunk is likely to pitch onto the floor.

Spend time finding out and memorising where everything is stowed, especially safety equipment – flares, safety harness and lifejackets. This also applies to ropes, fenders and other boat gear which is often required in a hurry. Even the absolute novice can lend a hand fetching and carrying and putting things back for a busy crew whilst learning what they are used for. After all, the fitter's mate learns his trade by offering up the right tools and watching them being used.

When everything has been stowed there is likely to be a call to put the kettle on. The gas is turned on at the bottle, which should be housed in its own separate compartment with an air vent outboard, although there may be another gas tap between the bottle and the stove.

70

Because gas is heavier than air, it is positively dangerous to turn on the gas at the stove and then strike a match. Always put a light to the burner first and *then* turn on the gas. If the gas is turned low on a boat there is a greater risk of a gust of wind blowing it out than there is in your own home, so keep an eye on it. Water and gas are both limited on a boat and are very heavy things to carry. The inconvenience of running out of either at sea will be obvious, so you will be unpopular if you boil more water than is needed. The gas should be turned off at the bottle whenever it is not going to be needed, especially when sailing. When a boat heels it is easy for someone to fall against the cooker and accidentally turn on a tap.

Sooner or later you will want to use the lavatory, and if you are not familiar with the working of a sea lavatory or the particular type on board, ask for a demonstration. Whatever the manufacturers may say, they are temperamental creatures.

Unless they are operated correctly they refuse to flush or empty, become blocked, or overflow. Because they are sea-water flushed, they constitute a potential risk of flooding the boat. They all have a sea cock on both the inlet and outlet pipes, and these are usually kept closed when the unit is not in use.

The No. 1 rule is that nothing is put down the loo which has not been digested, other than the minimum amount of approved grade lavatory paper. Even cigarette ends and matches will jam the valves.

A sea lavatory needs to be kept scrupulously clean if below decks accommodation is to be free from unpleasant smells. This is a chore which will earn you the admiration and gratitude of your fellow crew members if you should choose to take it on.

Before leaving this delicate subject it is well worth mentioning that constipation is a chronic complaint on cruising boats because people cannot come to terms with the mechanics of the sea lavatory and feel unnecessarily inhibited by the lack of privacy on board. An uninhibited crew is a happy crew.

Another piece of equipment which requires regular attention is the auxiliary engine. Before any trip, fuel and oil levels and stern gland greasing must be checked and the whole engine looked at for leaks in fuel or oil lines. Then the engine should be run until it is warm, and a check made that cooling water is coming out at the exhaust which shows that it is circulating. Then see that the temperature gauge is giving a normal reading and that the ammeter is showing a charge to the battery.

The level of the electrolyte fluid in the battery or batteries needs to be checked. This is often forgotten for long periods, and although batteries will continue to work with the level low they will not take or hold a full charge and their life will be shortened.

Left The companionway steps leading down from the cockpit have been swung to one side to give access to the engine. The engine instrument and switch panel is just inside the companionway within easy reach of a single-handed crew in the cockpit.

Right How long before we can be on our way, skipper?

It is not unknown for an engine to be started with the cooling water inlet cock still closed – as it should be when the boat is left. A few minutes of running without the cooling water circulating will completely ruin any engine. The only exceptions are air-cooled units, but they are not common as auxiliaries on sailing boats.

The engine should always be run for a few minutes before sailing even if it is not intended to use it just to make sure that it will start and run should it be needed. Every member of the crew must know where the engine switches on, how the gear and throttle controls operate, and how to stop the engine – particularly in the case of a diesel which cannot be switched off with an ignition key like a car.

There are still a few owners who ignore their engines in the honest belief that they are an unnecessary smelly weight in a sailing boat. They are the purists. To the majority of boat owners an engine is a blessing and an indisputable aid to seamanship. There is no sense or pleasure in spending hours in discomfort battling against adverse winds in a heavy sea when an engine will bring you quickly to shelter and comfort. Boats are for enjoyment and for going places. If the wind will not get you there, why not use the engine? Holidays do not last for ever.

Above all an engine is a safety device. Who wants to spend a rough night at sea with his wife and children because wind and tide are against him when he could motor home? And, in extremis, when someone is ill or you have lost your mast, where are you without an engine?

The ability to maintain a marine engine, diagnose faults and put them right without always calling in a mechanic (of which there are none at sea) is as much a part of seamanship as the ability to handle sails. The engine owner's manual should be kept on board and be required reading for all the crew at some time when they are resting from their more romantic labours of sailing.

When everything has been stowed below and the accommodation tidied up, when the peculiarities of the loo have been explained, and the engine checked and started, when the kettle is boiling or perhaps a bottle opened, what has been forgotten?

Perhaps the burgee and ensign – if it is still daylight. In harbour when the owner is on board they are hoisted at 0800 in the summer (25 March to 20 September) and lowered at sunset or 2100, whichever is the earlier. If the owner is not on board only the ensign is worn. The ensign is always worn in coastal waters, but on an ocean voyage would only be hoisted when passing another vessel. The burgee is left flying when sailing, day or night, because it shows the direction of the apparent wind. It is the custom nowadays to leave the burgee up all the time that the owner is in effective charge. Flag etiquette is all part and parcel of seamanlike behaviour.

Is there an occasional thump on the side of the boat? It is probably the tender which has been left streamed out on its painter. The boat will lie more to the tide than to the wind, but the tender will lie more to the wind and, therefore, may get blown against the boat. It should lie alongside the boat secured fore and aft, and with fenders out if it is not an inflatable. Painters should be brought inboard through fairleads and belayed to cleats or other fixed points.

Belay is an old, but perfectly acceptable, word meaning to make fast a rope. If a cleat is used the painter should be secured by leading it round the inboard end of the cleat, taking a full round turn and then two or more figures-of-eight and a final round turn. If a painter is secured to a part of the pushpit, a stanchion or a guardrail, then use a round turn and two half-hitches.

Pushpit, fairlead, cleat – new names, and there will be many more to learn when getting ready to sail. The time has come to make a tour of the deck and cockpit and to introduce you to some more gear and equipment.

A round turn and two half hitches.

7. Getting ready to sail

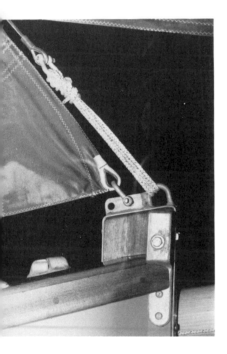

The very simple stem head fitting on a gaff rigged yacht built to a traditional design. The forestay is tensioned by a rope lanyard, and the tack of the headsail is shackled directly onto the stem head fitting.

Now the boat has to be got ready for sailing. The most important factor is the wind strength, which will determine the amount of sail which will be hoisted.

The latest weather forecast will have given an indication of the wind strength in your area, but that area covers several thousand square miles, the information may be some hours out of date and will be more accurate offshore than it is near the coast where the shape of the land can produce completely different local conditions.

The wind out at sea is almost always stronger than it is inland, and in the shelter of a harbour or marina it may be difficult to judge what it is like outside. If another boat has just sailed in, the crew will be able to supply the right information, or it may be possible to see other boats out sailing and estimate the wind strength from the way they are behaving.

If there are a lot of white horses (breaking wave tops) on the water outside there will be a fresh to strong wind blowing–too strong for a novice crew. But you may be the only novice and the others will want to go. It means getting your oilies on and being prepared for an exciting sail.

Having made his own assessment of the wind strength and sea conditions, the skipper will decide which sails to use. The mainsail will almost certainly be already bent on the boom and furled under a mainsail cover. The choice is whether to use the full main or start with it reefed down, and which headsail to set. It is better to set out with reefs in the main and have to shake them out later, than to start with full sail and find that the boat is over-canvassed when at sea.

A well equipped cruising boat will carry a minimum of three headsails–genoa, working jib and storm jib.

The genoa is a much larger type of jib which, when set, reaches well aft of the mast, in some cases almost to the front of the cockpit. It is a standard racing sail, and is used on cruising boats to get

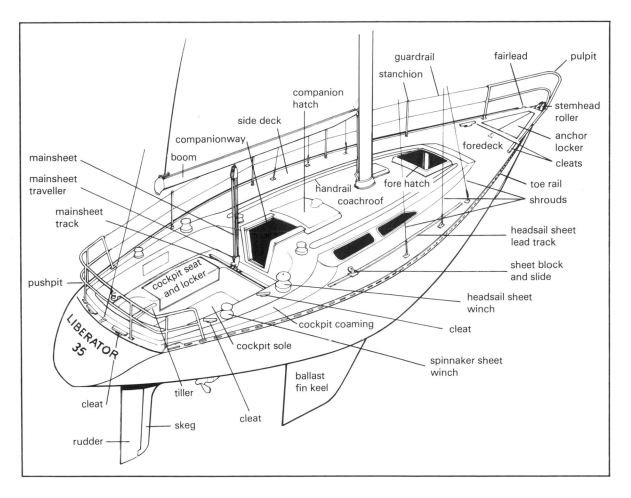

Liberator 35. The different parts of a boat's deck, cockpit and fittings.

a good drive in wind forces up to about 3 or 4. Above that the boat may be overpressed and the genoa will be changed for the working jib.

The working jib, as its name implies, is the general purpose sail which, on a sloop, just about fills the triangle between the mast and forestay.

The storm jib is a very small sail which, as its name implies, is used in really heavy weather.

Hopefully your first sail will be on a fine day with a gentle breeze blowing. The skipper will want to give you an easy sail rather than a fast one and will probably decide to use the working jib and full main.

The first job, if not already done, is to hoist the burgee, a small triangular flag, at the masthead. This shows which way the wind is blowing; in harbour or on a mooring it is the true wind. The burgee stick is attached to its own halyard by two clove hitches with

Left A very typical masthead arrangement with the halyards passing over pulleys built into the top of the mast and running down inside the hollow section and out through pulleys at the foot of the mast.

Right The traditional method of setting a headsail on a bowsprit. The tack of the sail is shackled to a traveller ring which is sent out along the bowsprit and hauled back in again by means of a rope passing round a pulley.

The basic sails carried by a cruising boat.

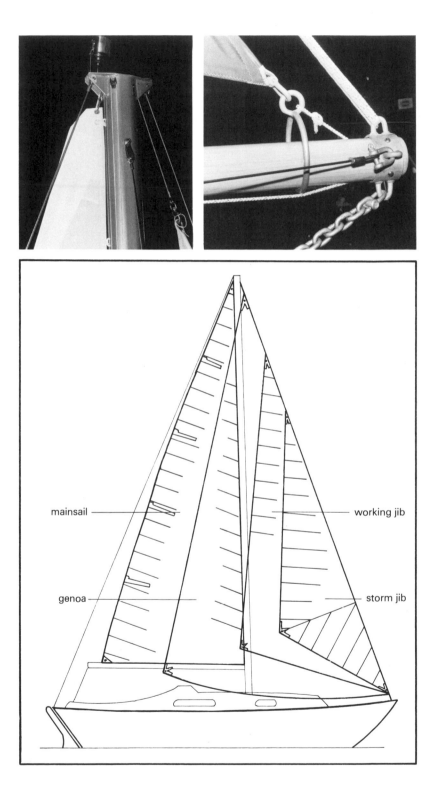

mainsail

working jib

genoa

storm jib

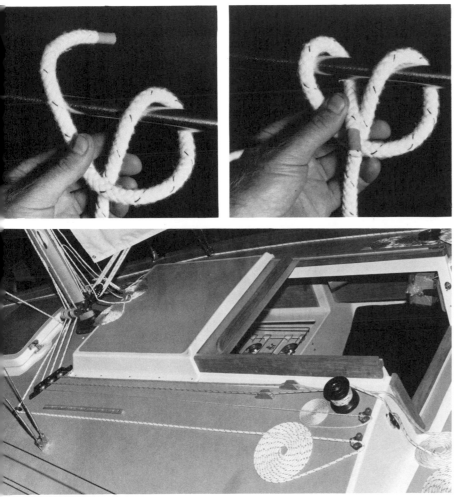

Above The clove hitch is used to secure a rope to any object, and is formed by making two half hitches and bringing the end of the second one through its own part. This knot is used to attach the stick of a burgee to its halyard, and is also a quick and secure way of attaching fenders to guardrails. But it can jam up tight under tension, so it should not be used to support any heavy weight or for chain.

Below The modern tendency is for halyards to be led back to a winch and cleats on the coachroof by the cockpit to reduce the amount of work which has to be done on deck.

the upper hitch being sufficiently low down the stick to allow the burgee to stand proud of the masthead.

Before hoisting it make sure that the halyard is clear of all obstructions and is running free with no twists in it. Watch the burgee as it goes up to see that it does not foul anything, then secure the halyard to its cleat on the mast.

The headsails will be in sail bags which, on most cruising boats, are stowed in cockpit lockers. The appropriate bag is taken onto the foredeck and tied to the pulpit or the guardrail to prevent it blowing away when the sail is taken out of it.

If the sail was bagged correctly after it was last used the tack will be at the top of the bag so that it comes out first and can be immediately attached by a shackle either directly onto a stem-head fitting or to a strop or tack tackle.

Above left Going forward with the sailbag. Prancing along the deck like this may be safe enough in harbour, but in anything of a sea it would be a sure recipe for being thrown overboard. Note the tack of the headsail is sticking out of the top of the bag.

Above centre The tack of the sail is shackled onto the wire strop at the stem head.

Above right Hanking the luff of the sail onto the forestay while keeping the bulk of the sail under control inside the sailbag.

Below left Attaching the last hank. The sail is now out of its bag, which has been tied to the guardrail to prevent it blowing away. The halyard is clipped to the pulpit rail so that it is ready on the foredeck and cannot be lost up the mast.

Below right Shackling the halyard onto the head of the sail. This would not be done at this juncture unless it was intended to sail straight away.

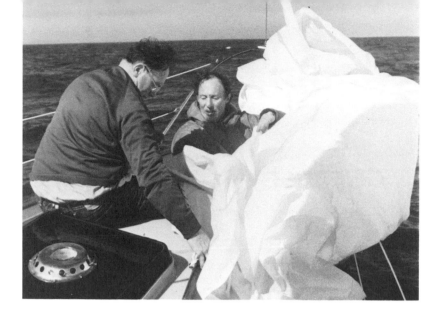

If it is attached directly to the stemhead, the foot of the sail could chafe on the pulpit or the guardrail when the sheet is eased. It will also block the helmsman's view forward on the lee side of the boat. A deck-sweeping genoa prevents wind from being lost under the sail and directs it more efficiently round the lee side thus increasing the drive. Low-footed headsails are, therefore, much favoured in racing.

But for the ordinary cruising boat a strop or tackle which puts the tack of the sail on a level with the top of the pulpit will allow for a much better view forward and to leeward, and the sail will not chafe and so will last much longer. A tack tackle serves the double purpose of raising the tack and providing a downhaul to tension the luff after the sail is set. How the tack can be set up will depend on how the sail has been cut by the sailmaker.

Once the tack has been secured the sail is captive and cannot be caught by the wind and be lost overboard. It can now be hanked onto the forestay, but work on the windward side of the sail otherwise if the wind catches it you will be smothered, and at sea you could be pushed over the side.

Put the lowest hank, the one next to the tack, on first and check that the luff is not twisted between the first hank and the tack. To make sure that you do not miss out any hanks, and that the luff does not twist, run a hand up the luff from one hank to the next. Check that the piston of each hank has gone home before going on to the next one.

When the whole length of the luff has been hanked onto the forestay get some tiers (short bits of rope or tape) or shock cords round the bunch of sail to stop it being blown up the forestay or over the side into the water. If the sail is not going to be hoisted for some time it can be lashed along the guardrail on one side clear of the foredeck.

A figure-of-eight knot.

Above At sea the headsail would more likely be handled from the sitting position.

Above and centre Securing a sheet to the clew of a sail with a bowline.
Below Two sheets rove through the cringle in the clew of a headsail and secured by bowlines.

If the headsail (jib) sheets are already set up on deck they only need attaching to the clew. If not they will have to be got out of their locker and led outside or inside the shrouds and stanchions and through their lead blocks on the deck and back into the cockpit. The skipper will have to show you how they run the first time. A figure-of-eight stopper knot must be put on the end of each so that it cannot run out through the lead block.

The tension on the leech and the foot of a headsail, and therefore the correct set of the sail, depend on the angle at which the sheet is led from the clew to its lead block. The best angle will vary with different sails and also, to a lesser extent, with sailing conditions. There will therefore be either two or more lead blocks on each side deck or a single block each side running in a track on the deck.

An alternative system uses snatch blocks which can be hooked into any one of a row of holes in a perforated toerail along the side of each deck. On cruiser-racing yachts there may be two or three tracks on each side deck to provide adjustment of the sheeting angle laterally as well as fore and aft.

The sheets may be two separate ropes, or they may be one rope seized (bound with twine) in the middle to form a loop with a thimble (metal eye) inside which is attached to the clew with a shackle. In the case of two separate ropes each must be shackled or tied to the clew with a bowline.

Shackles are the simplest attachment to use, but many boat owners prefer the bowline because a metal shackle on the end of a flogging sail can cause serious injury if it hits you in the face or on the head. The sheets must be rove through (passed through) the correct lead block for the particular sail being used.

Before attaching the sheets to the clew be sure that the foot of the sail is not twisted or caught up on any deck fitting. The sheets can be left attached and lying loose on the deck with their ends lying in the cockpit. The headsail halyard is not attached to the head of the sail until the time comes to hoist the sail. It is best left ready for use with its shackle clipped onto the pulpit or guardrail.

The cover on the mainsail will be taken off at this stage, and the only thing that needs to be said about that job is do not pull it off like a sheet off a bed. It will have to be neatly folded for stowing, and it is far easier to fold it up while taking it off the sail than to have it blowing about on the deck or in the cockpit.

Rigid tenders are usually left on the mooring when a boat sails because they are awkward to stow on board. If one does have to be brought on board it will probably need all hands to help, and the guardrails may have to be slackened off at the point where it will be brought in. The main halyard can be used as a

lifting gear to make the job easier. Before any tender is brought inboard it must be tilted sufficiently to empty out any water in it.

The most convenient place to stow a tender is on the coachroof where it is not taking up any working space. Secured right way up on a cradle or chocks it can be used as a stowage space for ropes, fenders and other gear, and also provide useful handholds for working on deck. But unless it has a fitted cover it will collect water. It is easier to secure it upside down, in which position it offers slightly less windage but it serves no useful purpose.

An inflatable is much easier to get on board and can be laid athwartships while being deflated. It is not good enough to open the air valves and expect it to deflate itself. It requires a little time and patience to get all the air out of the tubes, best done by kneeling on them. Any attempt to fold and roll up an inflatable before all the air is out of it will result in large pockets of air being trapped inside, and the package will be far too big to stow.

Another way of stowing an inflatable is to leave the aft section only inflated and fold the deflated bow section back over it. It can then be put overboard in an emergency and will support the crew in the water while the rest is blown up. This will only be possible, of course, if the bellows were secured to the inflatable when it was stowed.

Straps with quick-release fastenings or a web of shock cords are the two most popular methods of securing a tender on the coachroof. If rope lashings are used they can be tied down with a round turn and two half-hitches, which is quick and easy to undo. You should understand how the tender is lashed down in case you have to undo it and get it overboard in a hurry, which might be in the dark at night.

Above left The pick-up buoy of the mooring is left in the tender secured to the thwart by its line. The whole tender then becomes a nice big target to aim for when coming home.
Above right A sheet lead block on a slide with a spring-loaded plunger for adjustment of the block's position on the track.
Centre right A headsail lashed along the guardrail leaving the foredeck clear.
Below right Folding the sail cover while taking it off.

Above left Getting out of a tight corner: all mooring ropes have been cast off except a bow spring, which is left as a running line. The helmsman puts the engine into slow forward and the tiller over to starboard to bring the bow into the pontoon. One crew stands in the bows with a protective fender.
Right The bow is held in by her bow spring forcing the stern out.
Below The stern is now well clear and the engine has been put into reverse to take the boat out astern while the foredeck crew hauls in the running line. By reversing the manoeuvre and using an aft spring a boat can be swung out of her berth bow first.

When everything that stays on deck has been lashed down, and everything below decks has been stowed and all locker doors closed, you are ready to go.

From here on it pays to be completely honest with yourself and the skipper. Make sure that he is well aware that you are not experienced, and ask him to explain his intentions and what he is attempting to do at every stage. If you do not ask you will not learn. If he is a good skipper he will always tell you, but choose the moment to ask. Never distract his attention in the middle of a difficult manoeuvre or when he is trying to save a situation.

If you do not understand an order or how to carry it out say so and do not be frightened of making mistakes, but when you make them admit them. You will learn far more by making mistakes and discussing them afterwards than by playing safe and watching someone else do a job.

On your first outing in a sailing boat, if it is for your benefit, the skipper will in all probability motor out into open water before hoisting sails.

A boat is held in to its berth or alongside another vessel by mooring lines, and these have to be cast off before the boat can move. If leaving under engine all but two lines will be taken in and those two—one from the bows and one from the stern—will be looped round a bollard, mooring ring or cleat ashore with both their ends brought inboard so that one end can be cast off and brought back inboard by hauling on the other end without any of the crew having to be on shore. This system is called a running line.

Depending on the direction of the tide or the wind the skipper will order either the bow or stern line to be slipped first. If you are on one of them haul it in very smartly making sure that it does not trail in the water and foul the propeller.

Mooring lines are sometimes too long to coil in your hands as you haul in. Just let the line fall on the deck and tidy it up afterwards. When both lines have been slipped and the boat is well clear of the berth, bring in the fenders and get them stowed in their locker out of the way. Mooring lines are sometimes coiled down on deck on big boats, but on the average sailing cruiser there is not enough deck space, so they are kept in lockers.

Leaving an open mooring under engine is relatively simple as long as great care is taken that the line does not foul the propeller. Whoever is on the foredeck should throw the marker buoy and pick-up rope well clear of the bows, and warn the helmsman if it looks like going under the hull when the engine must immediately be put into neutral until the buoy is well clear astern. If there is sufficient room it can be safer to leave an open mooring astern and then go ahead and round the buoy.

If there is very little room for manoeuvre the pick-up buoy and line can be taken outside the pulpit and guardrails and dropped over the stern, while the engine keeps the boat creeping forward.

Left Getting ready to throw the pick-up buoy and mooring line clear of the bow.
Right By backing the headsail the boat can be made to pay off to leeward away from the mooring before the line is dropped overboard.

8. Leaving harbour-pilotage

If you are leaving a harbour which opens directly onto the open sea you will soon be able to hoist sail and experience for the first time the wonderful moment when the noise of the engine stops and the boat moves almost silently through the water propelled by an invisible force. If the sun is shining and the wind just right you will immediately appreciate why people love sailing.

More often it will be quite a long drive to open water, especially if your berth or mooring was up a river or estuary. There may be a channel to be followed, or hazards to be avoided – like banks, bars, rocks or wrecks; the fairway may be crowded with other boats, not to mention big ships. A tidal stream or strong current could be trying to set you off course all the time, and when you do reach the sea your movements in any given direction may be restricted by natural or man-made hazards until you are a long way out.

Fairways, deep water channels and hazards or dangers are all signposted with navigational marks – buoys, beacons, lights, bells as well as leading marks on shore – which are indicated on charts. The direction and rate of tides are also shown on charts, and in greater detail in tidal stream atlases, and there are pilot guides and sailing directions published for most popular yachting areas.

So the skipper has plenty of aids to help him, but unless he has local knowledge and experience he will have to do his homework before he heaves harbour and on the way out will be busy piloting the boat.

He may take the helm himself or prefer to have someone else steer the boat while he reads the chart, keeps a look out and gives instructions. Should you be given the helm you must execute every order exactly and immediately. There may be very little margin for error.

It is a time for concentration. For that reason if you are not on the helm do not distract whoever is with conversation. He

Above The way out of this harbour looks obvious—straight ahead past the spit of land on the starboard hand and then turn to starboard and out to sea. In fact as the buoys show, the channel turns 90° to port just after no. 3 buoy for about 3 cables and then 90° to starboard to the outer mark beyond the spit. One hour after high water a shingle bank uncovers as an extension of the spit, and a mud bank also uncovers on the port hand. At low water the channel is only a few yards wide off the spit. *Below* The effects of wind and tidal stream on boat, X, on a heading to pass outside the beacon, A, to avoid the area of outlying rocks between the shore and the beacon. If she continued on that heading she would make about 5° leeway, and her actual track over the ground would be towards B. Under the influence of a strong tidal stream her track would be towards C, but with leeway added she might well end up in the direction of D. Although the helmsman might keep her head pointing towards A, the boat would move crabwise over the ground towards D and would be standing into danger. To clear the beacon and make the open sea he has no option but to go to starboard and beat to windward against a foul tide. Until the tidal stream slackens or the tide turns he will make very little progress, if any, towards the beacon.

will need a clear view all round, so do not get in his way. You may be asked to go up forward and keep a look out; make sure you know what you are looking out for.

Steering a boat under engine is easier then helming a boat which is sailing. Just remember that if you are told to go to port you put the tiller over to starboard, and vice versa. If the boat has wheel steering then the wheel is turned in the same direction as you want the head to go. The response to the helm can be judged by watching the boat's head and seeing how much and how fast she moves in one direction or the other as you move the tiller.

There are three factors which can make a boat go off course even though you are steering in a straight line. The propeller has a transverse thrust. A left-handed propeller (turning anti-clockwise when looked at from astern) will tend to push the stern to port and the bows to starboard; with a right-handed propeller there is the opposite effect.

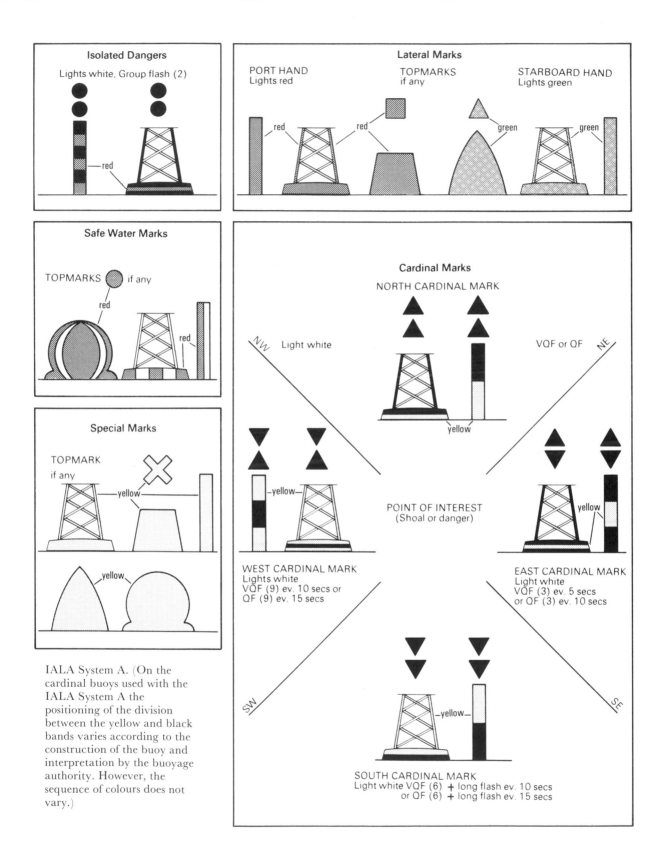

Isolated Dangers

Lights white, Group flash (2)

red

Lateral Marks

PORT HAND
Lights red

TOPMARKS
if any

STARBOARD HAND
Lights green

red — red

green — green

Safe Water Marks

TOPMARKS — if any

red

red

Special Marks

TOPMARK
if any

yellow

yellow

IALA System A. (On the cardinal buoys used with the IALA System A the positioning of the division between the yellow and black bands varies according to the construction of the buoy and interpretation by the buoyage authority. However, the sequence of colours does not vary.)

Cardinal Marks

NORTH CARDINAL MARK

Light white

VQF or QF

yellow

POINT OF INTEREST
(Shoal or danger)

WEST CARDINAL MARK
Lights white
VQF (9) ev. 10 secs or
QF (9) ev. 15 secs

yellow

yellow

EAST CARDINAL MARK
Light white
VQF (3) ev. 5 secs
or QF (3) ev. 10 secs

yellow

SOUTH CARDINAL MARK
Light white VQF (6) + long flash ev. 10 secs
or QF (6) + long flash ev. 15 secs

NW   NE   SW   SE

The tidal stream can affect the track of the boat over the ground, and so also can the wind. Although the head of the boat may appear to be pointing in the right direction, the boat can be crabbing sideways. The head may be lined up with the next mark which you are making for, but a glance astern may show that the last mark is not dead astern and that you are being set to one side or the other of the correct course which, if the safe channel is narrow, could put the boat aground or onto a hazard.

The limits of safe channels and the positions of hazards have in the past been marked by one of two buoyage systems – lateral and cardinal. In 1977 a revised buoyage system was agreed by the International Association of Lighthouse Authorities and, known as the IALA System 'A', it is now in use in all European waters – although there will always be local 'signposts' used by river and harbour authorities and yacht clubs.

The IALA system is divided into three groups of buoys or marks. Lateral marks are used to show the port and starboard sides or limits of navigable channels and are in the form of buoys or beacons. All port hand marks *as seen coming in from seaward* are red. Buoys are can shaped, and beacons have a can-shaped top mark. If they are lit they will show a red flashing light each with a distinctive rhythm. Approaching from seaward port hand marks are left to port, but when going towards the sea they are left to starboard.

Starboard hand marks are green. The buoys are conical in shape, and beacons have an upward-pointing cone top mark. If lit they will show a green flashing light. Approaching from seaward they are left to starboard, but when going towards the sea they are left to port.

In open water round the coast lateral marks are 'read' in a clockwise direction round continental land masses, which in the north west of Europe is basically from sw towards NE.

Cardinal marks are used to mark outlying and separated hazards and junctions and bends in channels, and are all black and yellow with distinctive top marks indicating their position relative to the hazard. At night they are distinguished by the rhythm of their flashing white lights. They are placed to the north, south, east or west of the hazard which they are marking. Their compass or cardinal position is indicated by the pattern of their black and yellow markings, but these are not always clearly visible against the light. The top marks, being shapes, are easier to see and to remember. North marks have two cones pointing upwards, and south marks have two cones pointing downwards. That makes sense. West marks have two cones point-to-point making a wine glass shape. East marks have two cones, one up and one down, base-to-base.

Above Buoys are not always easy to find in poor visibility. *Below* Taking a bearing with a hand bearing compass.

With lateral marks it does not matter in which compass direction you are going; you just leave them to port or starboard. But to read cardinal marks you must know the direction of north otherwise you will not know on which side of a mark to pass.

Isolated danger marks are used to indicate small isolated dangers with safe water all round, and are black with one or more horizontal red band and two black balls or spheres one above the other as top marks. At night they show a flashing white light.

Marks with vertical red and white stripes on a spherical buoy, or on a beacon with a single red sphere top mark, indicate safe water. A typical place to find one would be in the middle of a wide channel. Yellow marks are used for special purposes such as a military zone or a water ski area.

All marks are, therefore, identified in daylight by colour, shape and top mark, and at night by colour and rhythm of light. Lateral marks use red or green flashing lights, and cardinal and isolated danger marks use white flashing lights.

The light characteristics of navigation marks, including lighthouses, are given on charts using the following abbreviations:

V Qk Fl	— Very Quick Flashing (about 120 times a minute)
Qk Fl	— Quick Flashing (about 60 times a minute)
L Fl	— Long Flash (2 seconds or longer)
Gp Fl	— A series of 2 or more flashes separated by an interval. The number of flashes is given in brackets. Gp Fl (3) = 3 flashes in the group.
5 sec	— 5 seconds between each flash,
Occ	— Occulting light, one which is exposed for a longer period than it is obscured.

All the foregoing is known as System 'A' and is used in Europe, Africa, India, Australia and most of Asia. Another—System 'B' is being introduced on the North and South American continents, the Caribbean and parts of Asia.

Following the signposts, buoyage is only the beginning of pilotage, but it is often good enough to get you out of harbour and into open water where sailing can start.

But there are times when relying on buoys and beacons and hopping from one to another is not a sufficient or safe form of pilotage. They are not always easily seen in poor visibility; they can be out of position, especially after a storm; and the boat can be set off her course between buoys by a tidal stream, by making leeway, or both. Fixed objects on the land, provided they are marked on the chart, are all used in pilotage to check a boat's position by observation. One such object on its own has a limited value for estimating position by eye—a church tower will look the same over a wide angle of approach. A lighthouse on the end of a

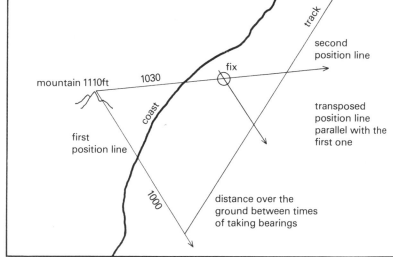

This conical shaped little mountain makes a most useful landfall mark. A bearing on its peak (which will be marked on the chart) will give a position line from which it can be determined if you are to port or starboard of your intended landfall. A more accurate position can be estimated by relating the position line obtained from taking a bearing with the point(s) at which the echo sounder indicates the crossing of one or more depth contour lines. The boat sailing parallel with the coast can get an even more accurate position by taking a running fix.

A bearing is taken and plotted as a position line on the chart with the time it was taken noted beside it. From any point along that position line draw a line on the same bearing as the boat's heading to indicate your track. After a suitable interval of time when the bearing on the summit has changed by more than 30° take a second bearing and plot that as a second position line. With a pair of dividers describe an arc from the juncture of the first position line and the boat's track with a radius equal to the distance over the ground covered in the interval of time between taking the two bearings. Mark where the arc cuts the position line. (The distance is taken from the log making allowance for any tidal stream or leeway).

Using a parallel ruler transfer or transpose the first position line from the first bearing to a position where it passes through the point where the arc cuts the track line. Where the transposed position line then cuts the second position line is a fairly accurate fix of the boat's position.

harbour wall seen straight ahead of the boat only tells you that you are approaching that harbour. But from what direction? If a compass bearing is taken on the lighthouse and the reciprocal (that is the bearing *from* the lighthouse) is plotted on the chart, the line drawn will show if your bearing will take you clear of danger.

Two bearings taken at the same time–one from the lighthouse and one from some other object such as a clearly defined headland–will give two lines to plot on the chart, and where they cross should be where you are. This is called taking a fix. Three bearings are theoretically better than two, but because of the time lapse between taking the first and third, and the fact that 100 per cent accuracy is rarely achieved with a hand-held compass on a moving boat, the three lines on the chart are very unlikely to meet at the same point but will form a triangle. The smaller the triangle the more accurate the fix.

Fix by transit and one bearing:
In this case the chimney and
the end of the harbour mole
in transit give one position
line, and a bearing on the
stack on the left provides a
second position line. The fix
is where the two meet, and the
time is always noted alongside.
The transit makes the fix more
accurate than a two-point or
cross bearing using either the
end of the harbour mole or the
chimney on its own.

Fix by three-point bearing:
Bearings have been taken on
the church, a tower on a hill a
little way inland, and a distant
lighthouse on a point. The fix
should be assumed to lie in the
corner of the triangle, or
cocked hat, nearest to any
possible danger – in this case
off lying rocks.

Position fix by one bearing and
a sounding:
Here a bearing has been taken
on a lighthouse on a headland
and the time of crossing the
10-metre depth contour noted
and marked on the chart. The
symbol for a depth contour
position is a double-headed
arrow along the contour line.

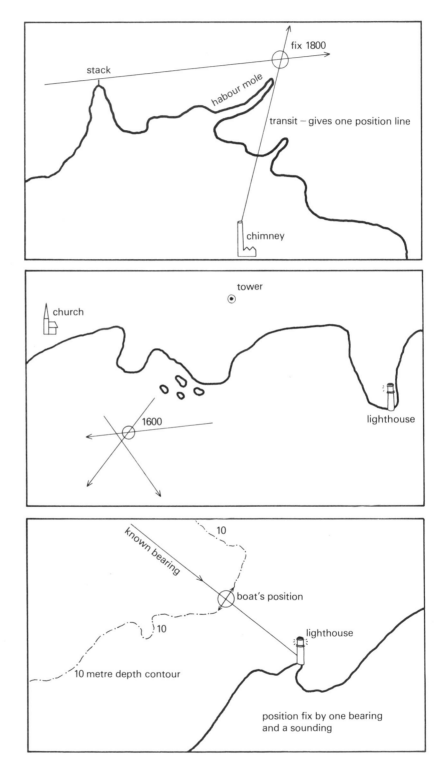

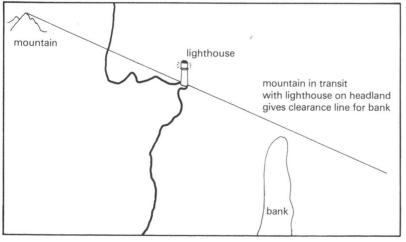

mountain

lighthouse

mountain in transit
with lighthouse on headland
gives clearance line for bank

bank

The lighthouse on Wicklow
Head see diagram below.
Using a transit to provide a
clearance line:
By keeping the mountain in
transit with the lighthouse on
the headland a course can be
steered to clear the dangerous
bank lying to port of the boat's
track.

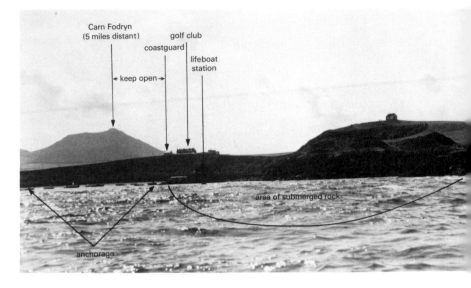

Carn Fodryn
(5 miles distant)

golf club

coastguard

lifeboat
station

← keep open →

area of submerged rock

anchorage

The anchorage in this natural harbour is immediately below the mountain five miles inland. The area of water below the cliff on the right is strewn with outlying rocks. There is no suitable transit to follow, but examination of the chart will show that by keeping the mountain and the buildings on the cliff in the middle ground 'open' a safe approach can be made to the anchorage.

Echo sounder and steering compass on a small cruising boat. The echo sounder is mounted on a hinged panel which allows it to be swung back inside the cabin when not in use. In wet conditions with the companionway hatch closed it is protected, but can still be seen by the helmsman.

A very useful method of position fixing is the transit—that is two objects which are in line with one another. There is nothing more accurate than the moment when two objects which had been separated come together along the line of sight. At that moment the boat is somewhere on a line drawn on the chart joining the two objects together and extended seawards. Two such transits must give an immaculate fix. It is sometimes possible to steer a straight course at right angles across a strong tidal stream by continually adjusting the helm to keep two objects—like a pier-head and a church—in transit. The channel into a harbour is often marked by navigation marks in the form of two transit marks set up on the land.

A fairly accurate position can be found by taking a bearing on an object ashore and reading the echo sounder (depth gauge). The bearing is plotted on the chart and the moment noted when the boat reaches a depth contour line on the chart. Where the bearing crosses the contour line is the position of the boat. However, the depth shown on the contour line is only correct at low water spring tides. At other times an allowance must be made for the height of the tide, so this method often provides merely a rough indication of the boat's position.

Large scale ordnance survey maps can be most useful when cruising along a coast as they give so many more land details, which can be used for taking fixes, than are found on charts. The wealth of detail on ordnance survey maps makes it much easier to recognise features on the land than it is from the sparse symbols on the land parts of charts. Map reading as well as chart reading make a passage along a coastline doubly interesting.

9. Hoisting sail

You are out at sea and—unless it is a windless day with a flat calm which is no good for sailing—the boat will have a pronounced movement. Until the sails are up she may roll from side to side in a beam sea or pitch up and down as she heads into the sea.

Until you have found your sea legs and the sense of balance needed to walk around and work on a moving deck, move slowly and very deliberately from one handhold to the next, and plant your feet down firmly at each step. Getting out of the cockpit onto the side deck calls for extra care because there is often a lack of convenient handholds in that area, it is a route you will frequently be taking, so work out a way which is best suited to your length of legs and arms. The same applies to getting back into the cockpit.

Always make your way forward and back again along the windward side of the boat; then you cannot be knocked over by the boom or headsail and, if you fall, you have the width of the boat between you and the water. Grab rails on the coachroof, the guardrails along the side of the deck and the shrouds are obvious handholds. As soon as some sail is hoisted the movement of the boat will become much easier and she will probably settle at one angle of heel.

Before the mainsail can be hoisted the boat has to be brought head to wind so that there is no pressure on the sail as it goes up, otherwise it would start to fill and blow out to one side making hoisting very difficult. Also the battens would foul the rigging with a big chance of breaking them or tearing the sail and, as that filled, the boat would start sailing before you were ready.

It makes light work if there are three crew to hoist the main—one in the cockpit, one by the boom on the windward side, and one on the main halyard by the mast. The crew on the boom takes all the tiers off except the one near the mast to keep the bulk of sail under control. The crew in the cockpit, probably the helmsman, uncleats the mainsheet which has been hardened in to keep the

HOISTING THE MAINSAIL

Left Freeing off the kicking strap.
Right Checking that the halyard is free to run.

Left Starting to hoist by hand.
Right The final hoist with four turns on the winch while watching the tension on the luff as it goes up.

Left Belaying the halyard on its cleat.
Right The halyard has been belayed, the kicking strap hauled taut, and the winch handle is now removed and stowed.

A safe working position when hoisting a mainsail at sea.

boom amidships, and eases it out. If the boom has been supported in gallows these must be lowered.

The crew by the mast hauls on the topping lift enough to take the weight of the boom and then belays it on its cleat. The other deck crew checks that the downhaul which holds the boom down at the mast end and the kicking strap under the boom are both free.

The man by the mast can then cast off the main halyard from its cleat and call to the helmsman to turn the boat head to wind. Whether he starts hoisting the sail by hauling on the halyard, or uses the halyard winch from the start, depends on the weight of the sail and the strength of the crew.

Hoisting must be done from the same side of the mast as the halyard and its winch, even if it is on the lee side. Otherwise the halyard will run at an angle through its block at the top of the mast and it will be much harder to hoist and it will chafe.

On a fairly large boat when the sail is well up the mast it will certainly be necessary to take a turn on the winch and continue hauling on the tail. Finally two more turns will have to be put on, and the winch handle used to get the sail up the last few feet. It is much easier if the crew who has been hoisting keeps hauling on the tail while someone else takes over the winching but, if working single-handed, he will have to winch with one hand and tail with the other.

Stop hoisting before the splice at the end of the halyard fouls the block at the top of the mast. Then the fall of the halyard is belayed on its cleat and the winch handle removed and immediately put somewhere safe. If it is laid down on the coachroof or deck it will surely slide overboard.

Above A simple way of securing a coiled halyard fall. A bight of the rope from the cleat is pulled through the coil, given a half turn . . . *Below* . . . and hung on the top horn of the cleat.

Above On this old gaffer there are no winches, so tackles are used and the final tension put on a halyard by swigging. *Below* Hauling a kicking strap down taut.

On boats which do not have a halyard winch, the sail has to be hauled up as far as possible by hand and then finally set up by swigging. A bight (loop) of the halyard is taken under the cleat while tension is kept on the tail. The halyard is then pulled away from the mast at right angles—like pulling a bow string—and the tail is given a quick pull to take up the slack which has been gained. This may have to be done several times to get the sail set taut. Swigging is often used with a turn round the winch to tension a halyard before, or instead of, using the winch handle.

When the mainsail is up, the topping lift is eased until the sail is taking the weight of the boom, and the luff is tensioned by tightening the downhaul. Some boats have a downhaul in the form of a tackle to get the gooseneck down its track; on other boats one of the crew has to put his weight on the boom and then lock the gooseneck in position in its track by a pin or by tightening up a locking screw. Finally the kicking strap is set up to hold the boom down.

When all that has been done the boat can be put on a course and the sail trimmed to keep her sailing while the person who hoisted the mainsail coils and stows the fall of the halyard.

Hoisting the headsail follows a similar procedure. The halyard is unclipped from the pulpit where it should have been left ready for use and, after checking that it is not twisted round the forestay or caught behind a spreader or crosstree, it is shackled onto the head of the sail.

The boat does not have to be brought head to wind to hoist a headsail, but it helps if the wind is well forward of the beam when there will be no weight on the sail as it goes up and the sheets can be left slack.

If the helmsman has to bring the boat towards the wind he should let the foredeck crew know which tack the boat will be on so that the sail can be moved over to the lee side of the foredeck. In that position it will not blow from one side of the deck to the other and either foul on something or smother the foredeck crew.

The tiers are taken off and the sail hoisted in exactly the same way as was the mainsail. The luff must be set up tight but not so hard that it—and not the forestay—is supporting the mast.

As soon as the headsail is up the cockpit crew must quickly haul in the slack of the lee sheet to quieten the sail, which will be flogging about in the wind, and then get it trimmed.

So much for the gymnastics of getting the sails up. What is the boat doing meanwhile?

If the headsail was hoisted with the wind forward of the beam the boat will be sailing to windward, but perhaps not very efficiently until the sails have been trimmed.

HOISTING THE HEADSAIL IN LIGHT AIRS

Left The skipper has motored out of harbour and decided to start sailing under headsail only. The foredeck hand starts hauling on the halyard . . .
Right . . . until the whole of the luff is up.

Left He then takes two turns on the winch and holds the halyard in tension by passing the fall under the cleat while he puts in the winch handle. He should have put three or four turns on the winch so that he could have tailed the halyard without using the cleat. If the headsail had to be taken off later in a strong wind it would be difficult to control the halyard as it ran out with only one full turn on the winch.
Right Setting the headsail luff up hard with the winch.

Left The halyard has been belayed on its cleat and the fall is being coiled. Note the end of the halyard is rove between the legs of the cleat with a figure-of-eight stopper on its end to prevent it running out and up the mast if the crew should accidentally let go the tail after casting it off the cleat.
Right The crew is about to secure the coiled halyard by taking a bight of rope through the coil and hanging it on the top horn of the cleat.

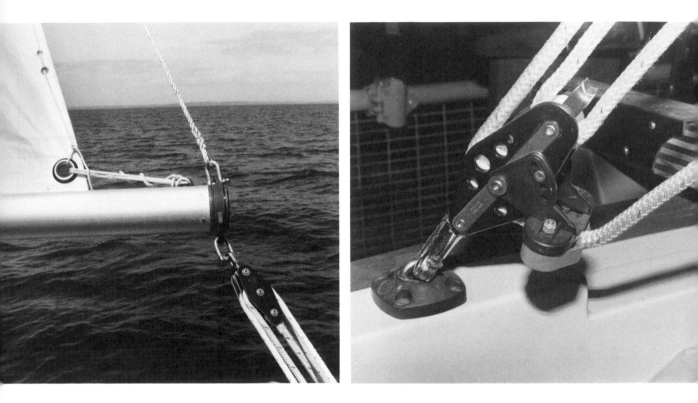

Left The outboard end of the main boom. The foot of the sail slides in a longitudinal groove and is hauled taut by a rope tackle. The topping lift and the sheet block are shackled to a collar which allows the boom itself to revolve to furl or reef the mainsail.

Right A mainsheet block with jam cleat. When the sheet has been let out or hardened in the tail is jammed in the cleat to stop it running out. When the sheet has to be adjusted again a sharp tug downwards will un-jam it.

The sheets are used to trim the sails by controlling their position relative to the centre line of the boat. It would be impossible to control the mainsail when it was filled by using a single rope from the boom to the cockpit. The mainsheet is, therefore, made up as a multi-whip purchase with the upper block attached to the boom and the lower block to the boat. The fall or tail of the sheet emerges from the lower block and is led to a cleat.

In some boats there is a jam cleat on a fitting alongside the block; in others there is a choice of two or more cleats in the cockpit. The lower block is normally attached to a slide running in a sheet traveller to provide a lateral adjustment of the sheet angle and its downward pull on the boom.

10. Tacking and gybing

Tacking is the manoeuvre which exercises a crew more often than any other. Except on a long passage at sea with a constant wind, a boat must frequently change course. Minor changes of direction can be made on any one tack by altering the trim of the sails, but the difference will be only a few degrees.

Since it is impossible to sail directly into the wind or nearer than 45° with most boats, a point to windward can only be reached by making a series of turns through the wind (tacks), bringing it first on one side of the boat and then on the other. In simple terms, a zig-zag course sailing at about 45° or more off the wind on each leg.

Tacks may also have to be made to avoid such obstacles as a headland, shoal water, rocks or other vessels. A classic example is a boat sailing down a river against the wind. She cannot sail straight into the wind, so she has to close tack first towards one bank and then the other until she reaches open water.

To bring the wind from one side of the boat to the other the head must pass through the dead sector where, with the wind blowing on both sides of the sails, the boat should come to a stop. The only thing that will get her through is her own momentum. It is therefore essential to get a good way on the boat (movement through the water) before starting to tack. If the boat is close hauled in light winds it may be necessary to first bear away onto a faster point of sailing, probably a reach, to gather speed before starting to tack.

It is the helmsman who decides the exact moment and gives the order. First he must look around to make sure that the water is clear in the area he will tack into. At the end of a tack the boat will be sailing at approximately 90° to her original course and on the opposite tack. If she is sailing on the port tack she will turn 90° to port and sail off on a starboard tack. If the helmsman does not look behind him and there is a boat coming up on his port quarter he will cut right across her bows and risk a collision.

THE TACK

Left Close hauled on the port tack.
Right Starting to luff up.

Left Head to wind. Both sails lie slack fore and aft.
Right The boat has passed through the eye of the wind. The boom has gone over to port, and the mainsail is beginning to fill. The headsail has gone over and is blowing out to leeward because the crew have been slow to haul in the sheet.

Left The boat is now sailing on the starboard tack, but the headsail sheet has still to be hardened in.
Right The manoeuvre is complete, but the boat has gone about more than 90° and is now more on a close reach than close hauled. The headsail sheet needs hardening in more. (Note the position of the copse on top of the hill which indicates the boat's change of direction.)

When he has checked that he has room to tack he warns the crew of his intention by calling out 'ready about'. This is an order to the crew on the sheets and a warning to anybody below, particularly if they are working in the galley, that the boat is about to heel over the other way.

The crew then makes a quick check that the sheets are clear to run and that the headsail is not likely to foul on anything as it goes over from one side of the boat to the other. When satisfied that everything is clear he uncleats the lee sheet and tells the helmsman 'all ready'.

The helmsman puts the helm down to leeward and calls 'lee-oh'. As the boat starts turning head to wind the crew takes the turns off the winch and lets the sheet fly, but ensuring that it is free to run out and does not get a kink in it and jam in the sheet lead block.

Meanwhile the helmsman moves across the cockpit so that he will be on the windward side on the next leg. The crew moves the other way and takes up his position on what will be the leeward side and starts to haul in the slack of the headsail sheet on that side.

As soon as the headsail has moved over the centre line of the boat he must get one turn on the winch and pull in the slack of the sheet before putting two more turns onto the winch as the sail starts to fill and put weight on the sheet. If more than one turn is put on the winch before the wind puts weight on the sheet they may over-ride each other and jam. Should he be too hasty and the sail is sheeted in before it has come across it will fill with wind on the wrong side (it will be taken aback) and the bows will be pushed back onto the old tack and the whole manoeuvre will be aborted.

In that case the sheet will then have to be let go on the windward side and hauled in on the lee side again. By this time the boat will have lost most of her speed and may have almost no way on her. It will be necessary to bear away to gain speed before making a second attempt to go about.

On the other hand if the crew is too slow hauling in the sheet and getting it round the winch, the sail will blow out to leeward taking the sheet with it, and the crew will have a long job winching it in again.

When the boat is sailing on the new tack the crew trims the sail by sheeting it in using the winch with one hand and hauling on the tail of the sheet with the other. If he is lucky the helmsman will help by tailing while he winches.

While winching the crew must watch the sail to see when it is trimmed. He should work with his weight inboard from the winch and not crouch over the top of it, in which position he will

GOING ABOUT TACKING

Above The boat is on a broad reach on the starboard tack, and the crew are preparing to get into a close hauled position before tacking to change course. The helmsman has the main sheet in one hand and will start hauling it in, while the crew on the winch hardens in the headsail sheet.

Centre left The boat is now sailing close hauled and the helmsman is putting the helm down to bring the head into the wind, while the crew is taking the turns off the sheet winch.

Centre right The boat is now head to wind – the main sheet is lying slack from the boom which is about midships. The crew has let go the sheet on the port side, changed places with the helmsman, put two turns on the starboard winch, and is hauling in the headsail sheet.

Below left The mainsail has gone over and started to fill, and the crew now has four turns on the winch and is using the winch handle to harden in the sheet while he watches the headsail – in this case a genoa – to get it in to within about an inch of the spreader. The helmsman, who has brought the tiller amidships to steady the boat on her new port tack, is watching the mainsail and the burgee. This boat has a tendency to pay off the wind a bit at the end of a tack, so he is having to give her a little lee helm to get her more up into the wind.

Below right The crew is satisfied that the headsail is in hard enough and is cleating the sheet. But the boat has paid off some more so the helmsman has put his helm down further to bring her back up into the wind.

not be able to watch the sail or use the full weight of his body to get a good leverage on the winch handle.

With three crew—one on the helm and two to look after the sheets—the job becomes much easier. When the lee sheet has been paid out the crew on that side can pick up the winch handle and move over to the new lee side and do the winching, while the crew who has been hauling in the sheet does the tailing. With a big genoa in a strong wind it will need two hands to harden in the sheet. When the sail is correctly trimmed the tail of the sheet is cleated and the fall coiled down out of the way of everybody's feet.

The mainsheet remains cleated throughout the operation. As the boat is going to windward the boom will already be near the centre line of the boat, and as the head goes through the wind it will move amidships with no wind in the sail at all. Then as the head continues to turn, the boom will move over to leeward as the sail starts to fill on the new tack.

On a modern fin keel boat which answers the helm quickly the helmsman must bring the boat about at a speed to match the working pace of the crew. A long keel boat is slower to answer the helm and may have to be literally sailed round rather than spun round, and the crew will have to keep pace with the boat.

Dexterity at handling sheets and winches, changing from one side to the other of a steeply sloping cockpit without tripping over a pile of ropes and dropping the winch handle or getting in the way of the tiller, will come with practice. Beginners should practise in moderate winds and where there is plenty of sea room. Then if anything goes wrong the boat can be put back on its original tack, the mistakes discussed, and the manoeuvre started again.

Close tacking has to be done right first time or the boat may stand into danger. It is not the time for the novice to try his hand, nor should he sit around in the cockpit getting in the way. When things get hectic do not take offence if you are told to get below. But if you have had plenty of practice in open water then close tacking is the best way to perfect your movements and timing.

The other way to change tack is to wear the boat round until she is running before the wind, and then take the stern instead of the bows through the wind and turn up into the wind again until she is on the new tack. This is the long way round and involves a gybe which, in any strength of wind, is the trickiest of all manoeuvres under sail.

When a boat changes tack by going about she has to be sailing into the wind and, therefore, the sails will be sheeted in and under control the whole time. The boom moves over slowly with no

A good stance at the winch. He is watching the sail carefully, and working with his weight well inboard from the winch. He is also well braced against the coaming and the cockpit sole against a sudden heel of the boat.

GYBING

Left A gybe in light airs when it does not matter if anything goes wrong: Running on the starboard tack.

Right The stern is turned through the wind, and the main sheet has been hauled in bringing the boom amidships.

Left The boat has gybed, the boom has gone over and the headsail is beginning to fill, but the mainsheet has not been eased.

Right The mainsheet has been let out and the boat is now running on the port tack, but the starboard sheet of the headsail has not yet been winched in.

The headsail has now been trimmed and the boat is gathering speed on the new tack.

weight on it while the boat is head to wind, and it only has a short distance to travel from one tack to the other.

To gybe a boat must be running before the wind and the main-sail will be right out almost 90° to one side of the boat. If the wind should go round to leeward of the mainsail it will be blown aback and the boom will be sent hurtling across the boat and out to the other side. In strong winds a heavy boom can be lethal to anyone whose head gets in the way.

In any but the lightest conditions this puts a heavy strain on the boom, its mast fitting and the mast itself. If the kicking strap is not secured and hauled down tight the boom will lift up on its way over and hit the sloping backstay which, in strong winds, could cause a dismasting. The fully extended sheet system weighted with its blocks follows the boom in a great swathe of ropes looking for someone's neck to snub itself on.

Those are the horrors of an accidental gybe, or what is often referred to as 'gybing all standing'. It is safer if you are all sitting.

On the other hand a controlled or intentional gybe is a per-fectly safe and acceptable manoeuvre. The boat must be running before the wind and sailing upright. The helmsman calls out 'stand by to gybe' and one of the cockpit crew starts to haul in the mainsheet, bringing the boom over the quarter.

He hauls in on the fall of the sheet keeping a turn on the cleat so that if he should let the sheet slip or if a gust of wind takes it out of his hand it will not run out completely and send the boom crashing back against a shroud.

When the boom is well on its way in, the helmsman calls 'gybe-oh' and puts the helm up (to windward). As the stern goes dead into the wind the crew on the sheet hauls it in fast to get the boom as near to amidships as he can. If he feels there is still a weight of wind in the sail he can take a turn on a cleat to hold the sheet in until the stern has gone through the wind and the boom has gone over to the other side.

In light winds the boom will just flop across, but with any strength in the wind it will bang across. Ideally the sheet should be hauled in so tight that movement of the boom is fully controlled.

As soon as the boom has gone over, the mainsheet is paid out as fast as possible. Again, if the wind is strong there will be a lot of weight on the sheet and if the crew lets it run uncontrolled through his hands he is liable to get rope burns.

But the boom must not be allowed to slam across; this puts a heavy strain on the mast fitting and the mast itself, and the sheet is liable to go wild and wrap itself round something or somebody.

During a gybe the headsail is not handled in the same way as on a tack. As the stern goes through the wind the headsail will collapse, but the sheet is not immediately cast off. It is eased out

GYBING

Above Running on the port tack, the helmsman calls 'stand by to gybe', and the crew starts to haul in the mainsheet.

Centre left With the boom on its way over to the centre of the boat the helmsman calls out 'gybe-oh' and puts the helm down.

Centre right The crew has hauled the main sheet in to bring the boom amidships.

Below left The stern of the boat has gone through the wind, the mainsail has started to fill again, and the crew is paying out the mainsheet.

Below right The boom is well over and the sheet eased out fully. The helmsman has brought the tiller amidships to steady the head on the new (starboard) tack. Throughout the manoeuvre the headsail has been ignored. In such light airs it is unlikely to fill and be effective unless it is goosewinged out on a whisker pole.

by hand as the sheet on the other side is hauled in. If the first sheet is let go the headsail can be blown over the bows and wrap round the forestay. When sailing short-handed the headsail can be left to its own devices until the gybe is complete.

That describes the procedure for gybing with the main and headsail set in the normal way. It becomes a little more complicated with the boom held back by a preventer (a rope from the end of the boom to a point forward on the deck) to stop it swinging about or accidentally gybing, and when the headsail is held out on the end of a whisker pole on the opposite side to the mainsail, a set-up known as a 'goosewing'.

On the call 'stand by to gybe' one crew has to go up to the mast and unship the whisker pole and stow it on deck during the gybe, and then set it up again on the other side after the gybe is complete. The same crew or another one has to undo the inboard end of the preventer and bring it aft outside everything and across ready to set up on the other side. The helmsman must be told when everything is ready.

Boats tack more often than they gybe because when going to windward they have no option but to go through the eye of the wind. But that does not mean that there is more merit in tacking than gybing; in fact when going from one broad reach to another the quickest way is to gybe. Some instructors do tend to over-emphasise the hazards of gybing in very strong winds when, if the whole thing is not carefully controlled, there can be dire results. Their words linger on in the memories of their pupils who remain apprehensive about gybing even in normal conditions when it is no more difficult or risky than tacking.

GYBING

Left The boat is on a broad reach on the port tack, and the helmsman has put the helm up to bring the stern through the wind to gybe onto a starboard tack. The crew is starting to haul in the mainsheet.
Centre The mainsheet has been hauled in to bring the boom near enough amidships, and the helmsman is waiting for the stern to go through the wind.
Right The stern has gone through the wind, the boom has gone over to port, and the crew has let the mainsheet out again. The helmsman is centring his tiller to steady the boat for a run on the starboard tack. Note that the wind is now behind the ensign.

Setting up a spinnaker boom as a whisker pole to wing out a headsail on the opposite side to the mainsail on a dead run.

To sail with the wind dead astern and the sails out at right angles to the boat is, in theory, comfortable and easy. The boat goes with the waves instead of slamming into them, there is no leeway, the boat does not heel, and the wind seems very gentle.

It is, however, quite difficult to steer a boat dead straight downwind; she is likely to start yawing and then she is no longer a balanced shape. As the boat rolls over there is more drag on one side, the rig is off-centre and she tends to turn. Then she rolls over the other way and tends to turn in the other direction. If the sea then gets up, as it will if the wind increases, the boat can very easily be slewed off her course by the waves and no longer be dead before the wind.

In any one or combination of those circumstances there is a risk, however good the helmsman's control, that the wind will get round on the same side as the mainsail is set and the boat will then be 'sailing by the lee'. Should the wind get behind the mainsail even for a moment the result will be an accidental gybe.

In the first two cases the remedy is to play safe, harden in the sheets a little and go onto a broad reach so that the wind is coming from about 30° on either quarter. There will be no loss of speed, perhaps an improvement, and the boat will be much easier to control with no risk of a gybe unless there was a very considerable and sudden wind shift.

However, if the boat was running with the mainsail out to starboard, for example, there would be no problem in turning to port to bring the boat onto a reach on the port tack. But if the course alteration demanded that she had to go onto a starboard tack then she would have to be gybed to bring the mainsail over onto the port side.

Fortunately when there is a good wind it usually remains steady in one direction for a length of time, and so if a course is set keeping the wind a little over one quarter or the other, long runs downwind can be maintained without difficulty. If the wind does shift it will probably be a definite change, and the boat will anyway have to come off the run and go onto a beam reach or to windward. It is when the wind is very light that it tends to keep shifting just enough to threaten an accidental gybe and makes an occasional controlled gybe necessary.

Sailing close inshore round a headland and into a bay and then up a river mouth could well involve running and gybing, then going onto a reach followed by a beat to windward close tacking all the way—all in the space of an hour perhaps. That is why inshore sailing and coastal cruising are far more valuable to the beginner than being taken on long open sea passages with long legs on the same tack and point of sailing.

Running goosewinged with the mainsail set one side and the headsail set the other side so that the one does not blanket the other. The headsail is held out with a spinnaker pole to stop it collapsing, and the boom of the mainsail has a preventer rigged and secured to a point on the foredeck. The preventer is to stop the boom swinging about or gybing when the boat rolls.

11. Dropping anchor and weighing anchor

Sailing develops a good appetite and, for many people, a good thirst too, so even on a day sail the crew need to be fed. If there is no hurry to get anywhere it is pleasant to stop for a proper lunch rather than try to eat and drink while concentrating on steering the boat or winching sheets. It is a bit difficult laying out a picnic in a cockpit which changes its angle of heel every five minutes. Going into harbour, if there is one nearby, can take up a lot of time especially if the crew go ashore. It is usually more practical to find a sheltered spot to drop the anchor.

When choosing a place to anchor the two main considerations are the weather and the tide. If there is no wind or barely a sailing breeze and the forecast is 'no change' there is no need to find a sheltered anchorage. All you need is some water which is shallow enough for the scope of your anchor chain and clear of any main channel. If it is close inshore on an ebb tide make sure you will not go aground before you are ready to leave. However, if the wind was good for sailing it will not be very comfortable riding to your anchor in open water and you will want to find a sheltered spot.

The land should be between you and the wind, not the other way round; in other words, you need an offshore wind. If you anchor off a lee shore (with the wind blowing onto the land) and the anchor drags you may be driven inshore and go aground and, if the tide is going out, you will be there for a long time. Also with the wind against the tide the sea will be choppy, if not rough, and when it comes to leaving you will have to beat out with perhaps very little room for tacking.

The chart will show if the bottom offers good holding ground or if it is foul ground full of old mooring chains, dumped rubbish or underwater cables which may foul the anchor.

When the boat is lying to her anchor she will swing with the tide and/or the wind, and in an extreme case could describe a full circle of 360°. If the tide turns she will certainly swing 180°.

Approaching an anchorage. The headsail has been neatly stowed out of the way along the guardrail, and the required length of anchor chain has been ranged on deck (none too neatly, however) and the skipper now has to decide where to drop anchor. He will have marked a suitable position on the chart allowing for depth of water and nature of the bottom. In this case the area of the anchorage is clearly identified by the other yachts already anchored. The skipper will have to select a spot so that he remains clear of their swinging circles. A boat will swing on a radius of her own length plus the scope of her cable.

So the point where the anchor is dropped must be chosen to allow the boat enough space to swing to a change of tide or wind direction.

While still approaching the anchorage the anchor and chain must be got ready. The anchor chain is usually fed down a hawse pipe (chain pipe) into a locker below. When it was last fed down it will have piled itself neatly in layers which should run out freely. But with the movement of the boat the pile may have shifted and the layers of chain become tangled. It is better not to rely on it running out freely when the anchor is dropped, but to haul out the required length of chain in advance and flake it down on the foredeck.

The rule of thumb for the scope of chain required is a minimum of three times the depth at high water in the anchorage. In windy or strong tidal conditions four or five times the depth at high water is not too much. If an anchor rope is used instead of chain the minimum figures will be five and eight times respectively.

DROPPING ANCHOR

Above left The required length of anchor chain (cable) has been hauled out of the chain locker and belayed on the cleat so that only the right amount will run out when the anchor is dropped, the rest remaining in the locker.

Above right Lowering the anchor. This crew member would be better balanced to control the run of the chain if he stood astride it. Also, bare feet are not recommended when working with an anchor chain.

Below left The boat is drifting broadside to the wind. If this continues it means that the anchor is not holding.

Below right The cable has snubbed and, held by the bow, the boat has swung head to wind confirming that the anchor is holding. The wire on the deck runs from alongside the cockpit on one side and back on the other side. This is the safety line to which crew can hook the shackle of their safety harness lifeline.

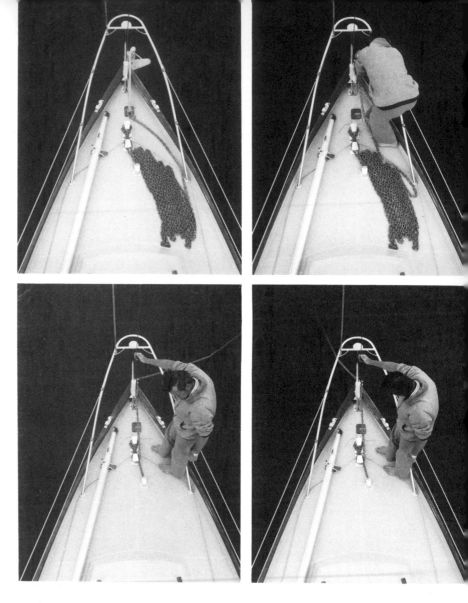

If the end of the chain is not already shackled onto the shank of the anchor that has to be done. The anchor can then either be hung over the bows with the top of the shank hard up against the bow roller, or laid with its shank on the bow roller and the flukes, or plough blades, sticking out ahead. It should only be hung over the bows in calm water, and then only while approaching the point where it will be dropped, in case it starts swinging against the bows and damages them.

The anchor is not dropped overboard and left to fend for itself. The boat will be brought up to the spot chosen with the minimum of way on her. It is up to the helmsman to judge when the boat is in the right place and to give the order 'let go'. At that moment the boat must be either moving very slowly forwards or have already stopped and begun to make sternway.

The crew on the foredeck can lower the anchor chain hand-over-hand or let it rattle out over the bow roller using the heel of his foot (with shoes on) to check it. If an anchor winch is used the chain is checked with its brake. The anchor must not be allowed to hit the bottom when the boat is stationary or the chain will coil down on top of it and foul it.

Dropping the anchor while the boat is moving forward, has its origin in Naval practice, but their ships are made of steel – or used to be. A yacht overriding her anchor is likely to get her paint work badly damaged. The preferred method, when possible, is to drop the anchor when the boat is going astern.

Once the anchor is on the bottom a couple of fathoms of chain are paid out and then checked (in a strong tide take a turn round an anchor winch, sampson post or cleat) to pull the chain up taut and dig the anchor in. In reasonable conditions it may be sufficient just to put a foot on it for a moment. The rest of the chain can then be let out and the inboard end made fast.

When belaying a chain, the load-bearing part must be at the bottom and the slack part at the top. If a turn of the chain coming from the anchor is put on last it will not be possible to take it off while it is under tension. The word 'chain' has been used because that is what it is. But a chain or rope secured to an anchor is often referred to as anchor cable.

After anchoring give the boat a few minutes to come to rest, and then take visual bearings on a couple of objects ashore to check the position of the boat. Two objects on the beam and in transit are ideal. If they open up the boat is still moving. A little later check those same bearings again; if they have moved you know that the anchor is dragging or that the tide has turned. Let the skipper know at once.

Except in an obvious anchorage among a crowd of other boats a black ball is hoisted in the rigging; if you do not have one a fender will do. At night an all-round white light is shown. These are international regulations for vessels at anchor.

When it comes to weigh anchor – either because it is dragging or it is time to move on – the boat has to be got ready to sail or the engine is started and left running in neutral. The foredeck hand, alone or with help, then has the hard job of hauling in the anchor cable until it is straight up and down but with the anchor still holding.

With a strong tide or wind and no anchor winch the skipper may have to be asked to help by motoring or sailing up to the anchor. When there is no wind or tide against you the anchor chain can be swaged by pulling on the chain to get the boat moving, waiting for the boat's way to carry her forward enough for the chain to go slack, and then pulling in the slack.

The anchor has been weighed and, while one crew member takes the weight on the chain, the other gets rid of the mass of seaweed clinging to the anchor.

Left The tripping line with marker buoy is bent onto the anchor and led outboard of the pulpit. The anchor will be lowered over the bow with the chain running over the stem head roller. The tripping line with its marker buoy will go over the side so that it does not foul the anchor chain.

Right There is often a certain amount of twist in an anchor chain, so the anchor rotates as it goes down and the trip line gets wound round the chain, which renders it useless. This can be avoided by keeping the trip line taut so that there is more tension on the line than on the chain.

As soon as the anchor cable is vertical the crew calls out or signals to the helmsman, and when the helmsman is ready to move the boat he gives the order for the anchor to be broken out. In some places, especially where there is thick mud on the bottom, this can be a back breaking task without a winch. The anchor may finally break out without warning, so always keep one leg braced behind you or you could end up flat on your back on the deck.

If the boat is being sailed away from the anchorage the skipper may have to act very fast the moment the anchor is clear, so he needs to be kept informed of progress on the foredeck.

The moment the anchor breaks out the rest of the cable and the anchor are got inboard before they can be overrun and scrape the hull. They may be covered with seaweed or mud, which will have to be cleaned off before the chain goes back down the pipe into its locker and before the anchor is stowed. Apart from the fore-deck being in a horrible mess, it will be too slippery to work on until it is cleaned up.

Before dropping anchor, if there is any doubt about the ground, a light tripping line is attached to its crown so that it can be pulled out by the flukes or blades if it becomes fouled. The line needs to be quite light, otherwise in a strong tidal current it may offer enough resistance to tug on the anchor and loosen it. It can be attached to a marker buoy just long enough for the buoy to float at high water or it can be brought back inboard, but over one side to prevent it tangling in the cable.

12. Mooring and coming alongside

If your first day's sail is on open water with plenty of sea room you will be able to concentrate on learning to crew without bothering about where the boat is going. The skipper will change from one point of sailing to another to give you practice at tacking and gybing and trimming the sails. There will be no need to stay too long on a wet beat to windward, or get frustrated punching a foul tide. You can go about and try another tack; you are in no hurry to get anywhere. The object of the exercise should be to give you a taste for sailing. As a result, at the end of the day you may begin to think that sailing is easier than you thought it was going to be. When the time comes to head for home you may have a chance to revise your opinion.

The skipper may no longer be able to take the soft option of choosing the easiest or most comfortable point of sailing. He will have to set a course for his home harbour or anchorage, which may mean a hard beat to windward with frequent tacks or a hairy run with the constant threat of a gybe. If the wind is against tide and both are strong it could be a very wet and uncomfortable ride. If the tide is against you you will be home a lot later than you anticipated. Only if the wind dies away will the skipper–if he is a good instructor–put the engine on and stop sailing.

Once you turn for home you will be sailing for real, not practising. It will be the time to put to the test what you have learnt during the day. The channel into the harbour may be tortuous and restricted, so orders will have to be carried out promptly. If the boat is going alongside or into a berth, warps and fenders must be got up on deck and everybody given their jobs to do.

Conditions inside a harbour are different from outside, so a sail may have to be taken off if the boat is going in under main or headsail only. There may even be a sail change which, at this stage, you may not have practised. In which case the skipper will have to do it and you may be given the tiller and quick instructions as to course. It is the time to keep a cool head.

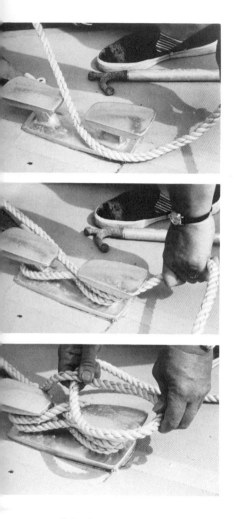

Belaying a rope round a cleat with two figures-of-eight and a half hitch.

Opposite Close hauled and heeled well over in the Bay of St Tropez.

In making landfalls and in what can be called close quarter work every situation is a little different and very often has to be handled by instinct—something which can only come with experience. But however experienced the skipper, however good his judgment, he must to some extent rely on his crew.

You may not always know why he makes a decision, but if you are alert and willing and carry out orders promptly and correctly when there is close quarter work to be done, you will be in much demand as a crew member. The last place to be when entering harbour is down below sorting out your socks or doing the washing up. That can all wait. The skipper might want all available hands on deck.

He may change his mind at the last moment because the mooring he was going for is occupied, or the space he was looking for along the harbour wall has been taken by a fishing boat. Nothing is certain when you come into harbour unless you have a berth in a marina, when you will almost certainly motor in. There comes a time when approaching a berth or a mooring when the skipper has to decide whether to continue under sail or put the engine on and get the sails off. In the crowded harbours and anchorages of today he will most likely decide to make the final approach under engine, especially if he has an all-novice crew.

Getting the sails off means lowering them and this may have to be done quickly. The skipper may want to take the headsail off first and then the main, or the other way round. or he may want to keep one up for a little longer. Before going on deck you must know his intentions, particularly if he is going to change tack because you will have to work on the windward side of the sails.

Take a few sail tiers with you looped round your waist or belt. Do not put them in your pocket because when you pull one out the lot will come out and scatter on the deck. If the skipper wants the mainsail off get the coiled main halyard fall off its cleat and lay it on the deck coiled down with the running part on top. If it is tangled up uncoil it and flake it down on the deck—a flaked rope is far more likely to run out freely than a coiled one.

When the halyard is ready to be uncleated tell the helmsman and ask when and how high he needs the boom to be hoisted by the topping lift. The hoisting of the topping lift involves getting the weight of the boom off the sail so that when the mainsail is lowered the boom will remain approximately horizontal. The mainsheet may have to be eased first. Uncleat the halyard—after making sure that the end of the fall is secured to stop it being lost up the mast when the sail comes down—and start lowering the sail.

At the same time the helmsman should let the mainsheet go free to spill wind out of the sail. If the sail needs help to come down, pull on the luff not on the leech, and use your arms to smother the

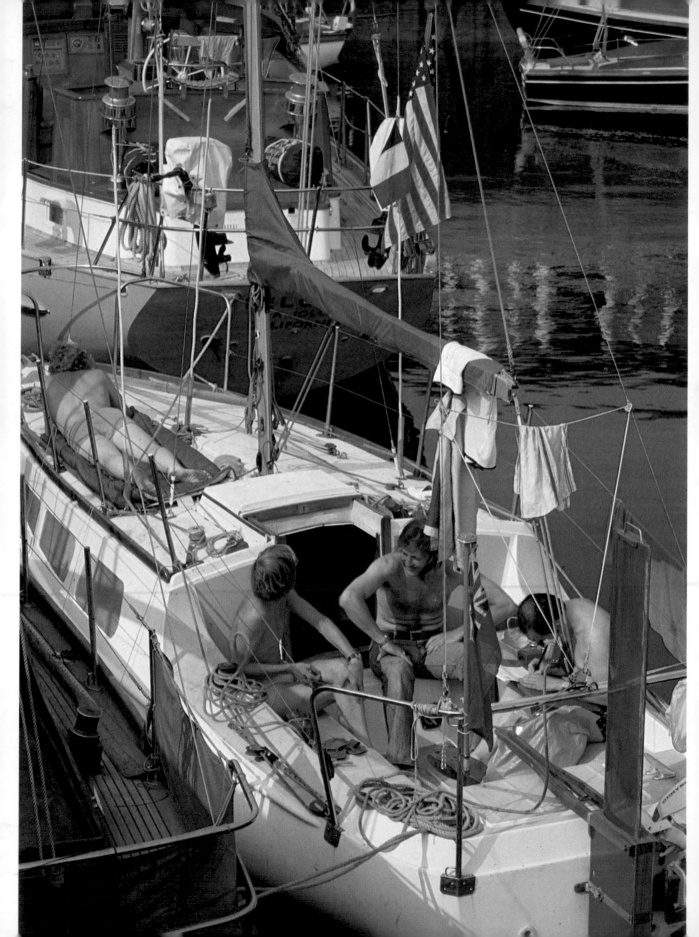

bulk. If the sheets are hardened in again to bring the boom near amidships the job will be made easier.

As soon as the mainsail is down it must be roughly stowed for the time being to prevent it flogging about. Get some tiers round it quickly. To be neat about it pull three or four feet of the foot of the sail away from the boom to form a bag or hammock into which the rest of the sail can be folded and then roll the lot on top of the boom like a long sausage, and lash it with your sail tiers.

The head of the mainsail should be unshackled and the halyard taken to the side of the boat and re-shackled to the guardrail. This will prevent the halyard from flapping and annoying other boat users. The downhaul and the kicking strap can be uncleated ready for rehoisting, the boom gallows set up – if used, the boom dropped onto them and the mainsheet fall coiled. But those are not immediate jobs; they can wait until the boat is tied up.

The easiest way to get a headsail down is to do it as the boat tacks. The sheet should be eased a few inches as the boat comes head to wind, and the halyard let go. The headsail will then fall down on the deck and cannot go overboard because it is still held by the sheet and the forestay. If the sheet is let fly the sail can land up half in the water, and if it is still on the winch and bar taut the luff will be pulling against the forestay and will not come down.

Left Getting the mainsail down by pulling on the luff.
Centre and right Getting the mainsail stowed on the boom and secured with sail tiers.

Opposite The blue water sailer knows no frontiers. Here an American and a British boat rest together in a French harbour after long passages.

Getting the headsail down.

As soon as the headsail is down, the sheet is hardened in again to stop the clew end of the sail from going overboard into the water and pulling the rest of the sail after it. The foredeck crew must gather in the sail as it comes down, get tiers round it, and secure it to the guardrail on one side of the foredeck. That way the foredeck is left clear for working on. The head of the sail should be held down with a tier to stop it being blown up the forestay, and the halyard taken off and re-shackled onto the pulpit; left on the head of the sail it can twist itself round the forestay.

Picking up a mooring whether under sail or power requires close co-operation between the helmsman and the foredeck crew. It is the helmsman's job to position the boat so that the mooring buoy is within easy reach off the port or starboard bow with almost all way off the boat. There is very little margin for error – either the buoy is within reach by boat hook or by hand, or it is not. The helmsman will normally try and sail up to the mooring into the wind, preferably under mainsail only, so that the foredeck is clear and he has a good view forward. He will luff up to take way off the boat when about a boat's length away from the mooring.

Very much depends on the strength and direction of the wind and tide and the characteristics of the boat. She must not be moving too fast for the crew to hold onto the buoy once he has hooked it, but she must be moving fast enough for the rudder to be effective so that the helmsman has steerage way. If the boat stops completely her head may be blown away from or over the top of the mooring, or she will start going astern.

The foredeck crew stands ready with the boat hook without blocking the helmsman's view. Communication between foredeck and cockpit may be difficult if the engine is running; it is then better to use prearranged hand signals. If the boat hook is held up-and-down in Navy fashion it can be tilted one way or the other to indicate to the helmsman that a port or starboard correction is needed. The crucial moment is when the bows block the helmsman's view of the buoy and he has to rely on signals from the foredeck crew.

There are two types of mooring buoy. The pick-up or marker buoy is the easier to moor to. It is attached by a rope riser to a heavy chain on the bottom, and it will usually have a pick-up

PICKING UP A MOORING

Above left Going too fast.
Above right Bang on target, but pity the foredeck hand! On a boat with a higher freeboard he would have no hope of reaching the buoy.
Below left Coming up alongside the marker buoy slowly and within boat hook reach . . .
Below right . . . and the marker buoy is hooked and brought inboard.

ring or loop on it which can be caught with the boat hook or in the hand. The buoy is then brought inboard, underneath the bottom pulpit rail, and the rope hauled in after it.

In some cases the boat can be moored by the rope riser which is led through a fairlead at the bows and belayed round a heavy cleat. In other cases the riser is used to haul in the chain off the bottom which is brought in over the stem head roller and secured by three turns round the mooring cleat without any knots or hitches. The turns can be kept secured by cleating the rope riser or making it fast somewhere so that it keeps a tension on the turns of the chain.

Whether a boat hook is used, or the crew lies on the foredeck and gets hold of the pick-up buoy with one hand, depends on the size of the boat and the height of her freeboard. If the boat hook is used it should be held with its hook facing upwards so that when its shaft is pulled in the buoy will remain on the hook. If the hook is pointing downwards the buoy is likely to drop off. Some people prefer to hook the rope riser just below the buoy and bring up a bight of rope with the buoy acting as a large stopper. If the buoy is being picked up by hand the rope under water may be the better target to go for.

The other type of mooring buoy is much bigger and is shackled to a heavy chain going down to the ground tackle of the mooring and it remains in the water. It will have a fairly large mooring ring on top of it which is caught and held with the boat hook then a mooring rope, with one end secured on board, is passed through the ring and brought back inboard and made fast to a mooring cleat. The mooring rope is led out and back either over the stem head roller or through a fairlead.

For a more permanent mooring, or if the mooring is not well sheltered, the anchor chain can be shackled to the mooring ring of the buoy or to a link in the rising chain under the buoy. The original mooring rope can be left in place as it will be useful when it comes to leaving the mooring again.

The only way to get ashore from a mooring is by tender and it may be that you will have to do the rowing. If it is an inflatable dinghy you will get nowhere fast by trying to row it as you would a conventional rowing dinghy. It will carry no way on it between strokes, and if there is a tide running or a wind against you it is possible to actually lose way between strokes. An inflatable must be propelled by very short quick strokes using a circular motion of the arms instead of long pulls. The blades remain vertical and work like paddles; they are not feathered. Do not forget your lifejacket and, even if using an outboard motor, take a pair of oars as well.

Before setting off from the boat, and also when returning from the shore, study the direction and strength of both the wind and tide and try to calculate how much they will set you off course. If other people are rowing to and from boats watch what they are doing. If you are on a mooring up tide of the slipway or steps you have to reach and you start rowing in a direct line towards them you may be swept downstream well past them and end up stuck on the mud or pinned against a harbour wall. You might even end up going out to sea.

Your course will have to be across the tide aiming upstream of where you want to go. If your landing place is up tide or up wind you may have to aim for a point down tide or wind to arrive in the right place. Except at slack water the direct route is very rarely the right one. The effect of wind is stronger with an inflatable dinghy than a rigid one. Before returning to your boat you might have to haul your tender a hundred yards or so to get up tide before setting off.

Crews who can manoeuvre their yacht under sail in a crowded harbour and put her alongside a harbour wall or pontoon without using the engine have brought their seamanship and teamwork to a fine art. It is unlikely that you will be asked to assist in bringing a boat alongside under sail in your early sailing days. In many popular yachting centres and marinas there is just not enough room to manoeuvre under sail without the serious risk of an insurance claim.

Before coming alongside a harbour wall or pontoon the skipper has to assess the strength and direction of wind and tide and any current before deciding his direction and angle of approach. While he is doing that the crew must make ready mooring ropes and fenders. As soon as it is known which way round the boat is going in fenders are distributed along the side of the hull which will be against the berth. They are often secured to the stanchions, although there are those who say that this is bad practice and that they should be on cleats. Unfortunately there are seldom enough cleats in the right places.

As the position of the fenders may have to be adjusted, it is important that they can be easily and quickly untied so their lines are secured with a round turn and two half hitches. It is well to have one crew member standing by with a spare fender to fill an unprotected point on the topsides. This is essential when going alongside an uneven wall or another boat, or if there is a swell and the boat is likely to sheer about after she has come alongside.

The bow rope and stern rope are always the first two to be taken ashore, and they are got ready first. A length of the bow rope is uncoiled and passed over the top of the pulpit and brought back inboard under its bottom rail, passed through the bow fair-

COMING ALONGSIDE

One of the crew stands by the shrouds ready to step ashore onto the pontoon with the bow rope.

Swigging on the bow rope to pull the head of the boat in.

The bow rope has been taken round a cleat on the pontoon and is being taken aft to act as a spring. This is acceptable for a temporary stop with a moderate size boat in calm conditions, but at least a turn should have been taken round the cleat on the pontoon.

A crew member with spare fender to fill an unprotected point on the hull when coming alongside.

A mooring rope belayed round a cleat. The rope should have been led through a fairlead instead of round the bottom of the pulpit rail. Fairleads, as their name implies, are provided to give a rope a fair lead so that it will not chafe or jam against some deck fitting.

lead and secured to a mooring cleat. The coiled end is then taken back to a point near the shrouds and either laid on the deck or coachroof or held ready to be taken ashore. The stern rope is passed over and under the pushpit in the same manner and secured to a quarter cleat.

The bow rope usually goes ashore first, and the crew with the rope waits until the boat is just about to touch, climbs over the guardrail by the shrouds and steps ashore. Having secured his bow rope he can go aft and take the stern rope which can be thrown or passed to him, if it has not already been taken ashore by another crew. It is better to get the bow secured first because it is difficult to get in if the wind or tide takes it, whereas there is a rudder and propeller on the stern to help get that in.

If a boat of any size starts to swing it is useless trying to hold her or pull her back by hanging onto the end of a rope. You can have anything from 5, 10 or more tons weight of boat pulling against you. But with just one turn round a bollard or cleat even a big boat can be held with a little weight on the tail of the rope. She can then be brought in a bit at a time by swigging on the standing part of the rope.

These two fore and aft ropes, which ought to be of equal length, are taken as far ahead and astern as is practical. If the boat is berthed around half tide their lengths need to be at least three times the range of the tide. If there are bollards on the quay or pontoon a bowline is made on the end of each rope so it can be looped over. With rings, a round turn and two half hitches will suffice for most situations, and on cleats a figure-of-eight finished off with a hitch.

Mooring lines are always secured ashore and adjustments made by the crew on board, hauling them in or easing them out. They always run through fairleads. After the boat has been positioned with the mooring lines, fore and aft springs are set up to hold her close in and stop her surging to and fro. The fore spring runs from the foredeck to a point on the shore level with the stern, and the aft spring runs from the quarter to a point

The rise and fall of tide in this harbour requires careful attention to the length and arrangement of mooring lines.

ashore level with the bows. When tying up alongside another boat your springs are made fast to her, but the fore and aft lines go ashore.

Breast ropes are additional lines sometimes run from fore and aft to the shore at right angles. They are an extra security and complication to keep the boat firmly alongside, but they cannot be used if the boat is left unattended in a tidal berth.

In tidal waters all mooring ropes need to be slack enough to allow for the rise and fall of the tide. In his home port the skipper will know exactly how to adjust the ropes to allow for the up and down movement of his boat, but in a strange harbour someone will have to stay on board to make the adjustments. The inboard ends of all lines are not finally cleated and the falls coiled down until the skipper is satisfied that the boat is lying as he wants her.

Lying alongside in a harbour which dries out calls for very careful adjustment of the mooring lines to keep the boat in to the wall as she takes the ground.

The problem is to ensure that when she does take the ground she leans over against the wall and not out the other way and so falls outwards. She can be made to heel towards the wall by shifting as much weight as possible over to that side. The anchor chain laid out along the side deck is the most obvious method, but spare fuel or water containers or any other fairly heavy and moveable gear can also be used. The most manageable weight is the crew themselves.

If the boat has to be left unattended a line can be rigged from the mast to the shore to hold her over. The spinnaker halyard is normally used to do this. It has to be long enough to be slack when the mast rises on the top of the tide, and short enough to hold the mast over when the tide falls. The technique is to hang a weight on the halyard to take up the slack. Having said that, the skipper who cares for his boat will never leave her on her own while she is taking the ground or when she is starting to float again.

13. An introduction to navigation

When you first go sailing your mind will be sufficiently occupied with learning the ropes and working out where the wind is coming from without having to worry too much about where the boat is going. You will be relying on the skipper to look after the navigation. You could continue day-sailing from one season to another without ever doing any navigation if you were content to remain a deck hand taking orders. But, unless you are only there for the fresh air, who wants to be just a deck hand?

Certainly before you can go cruising and play a full part as a crew member, let alone eventually take charge of your own boat, you will need to have a working knowledge of navigation. It is a subject which can be learnt at home or in the classroom, and the theory can be put into practice on the kitchen table using hypothetical situations. As was mentioned earlier, it is a good subject for study during the winter months.

Apart from a text book you will need some practice charts, a parallel ruler, dividers, pencil and rubber, tide tables, a nautical almanac and a tidal atlas.

Although you can learn to do specific jobs on board to help with the navigating–like taking compass bearings or making log entries–before you have learnt the theory, you cannot act as navigator until you have all the theory put together. So perhaps an introduction to some aspects of the subject might be helpful to you.

After considering the weather, the first question which has to be asked before putting to sea in many parts of the world is–What is the tide doing? The tide determines the depth of water in any one place and, therefore, where you can or cannot go, when you can leave harbour, and when you can enter another one. The speed and direction of the tide will determine the speed you move over the ground and the course you have to steer. Except in a few tideless seas like the Baltic and Mediterranean, you cannot sail anywhere without considering it.

Above Navigation is the art of knowing where you are. Approaching the harbour of Castlebay on the Isle of Barra from the east is a simple matter of taking bearings on a line of hills. From north to south – (1) is Ben Heaval (1,260 ft or 384 m) and (2) is Ben Tangaval (1,925 ft or 587 m) 2½ miles (4 km) further south. The entrance to Castlebay township and anchorage is through the Sound (3) and then turn right to below the southern slope of Ben Heaval. Vatersay Island (4) lies to the south of the Sound.

Centre There is Castlebay township at the foot of Ben Heaval . . .

Below . . . but when the Scotch mist comes down, as it often does, and without warning there is no Ben Heaval or any other landmark to lead you. The moral is that navigation must be practised all the time and dead reckoning kept up.

Tides are caused by the gravitational pull of the moon and the sun and are, therefore, fairly predictable. Almost everywhere there are two tides in every 24 hours, each with a high water and a low water approximately 6 hours apart. It is therefore falling for 6 hours, rising for 6 hours, and then repeating the cycle. There are local exceptions where the configuration of the land upsets this cycle and the periods of rise and fall may not be equal, and there may even be two high and low waters in a 12-hour period.

The range of a tide is the difference between the height of the water level at high and low, or low and high, water of any particular tide. The range will change from tide to tide between new moon and full moon. At full moon and at the last of the old and the first of the new moon the range will be at its greatest. They are called spring tides when high tide will be very high and low tide will be very low, and the tidal stream will flow at its fastest.

At the time of the half moon, waxing and waning, the range will be at its smallest so high tide will be much lower and low tide will be much higher than at springs, and the tidal stream will be flowing at its slowest. They are called neap tides. The range of tides increases daily between neaps and springs and is then said to be making, and it decreases daily between springs and neaps and is said to be falling. When the tide is rising it is said to be flooding, and when it is falling it is ebbing.

The predicted times of high and low water for all major ports, together with the tide levels, are listed in Admiralty Tide Tables, Reed's Almanac and similar publications in all other countries. The lengths of times to be added or subtracted for places between those main ports are also given. Local pocket-size tide tables are often available, and are particularly useful for working out the best departure or arrival times for your next trip while still at home. If you know the time of high water and the tidal range, the depth of water at any time before or after high water can be roughly estimated by dividing the range into six parts and applying the following table:

In the 1st hour the tide will rise or fall	1/12th of its range
2nd	2/12th
3rd	3/12th
4th	3/12th
5th	2/12th
6th	1/12th
6 hours	12/12th

Tidal changes result in the movement of water from areas of high water to fill areas of low water, and then back again. This movement or flow of water is called the tidal stream, and its direction of flow is called the set of the tide. The speed at which it flows is the rate of the stream and is always given in knots (nautical miles per hour). 1 knot or nautical mile = 1.152 statute miles. The rate and set of the tidal stream are of paramount importance when sailing because together they directly affect both the speed and the course of the boat over the ground.

Over the ground is the important point to remember. The tide does not affect the speed or direction of a boat *through the water*. To understand this you must visualise the sea as a solid mass of water moving in one direction or another over the top of the sea bed. A boat floating on top of that mass of water is carried forwards, backwards or sideways in whatever direction the mass of water is moving and at whatever speed it is moving. But she is still free to move in any direction and at any speed through that water, in exactly the same way as a man can walk quickly or slowly, backwards, forwards or sideways on the deck of a boat regardless of the direction in which she is carrying him.

The rate and set of the tidal stream can be found for a limited number of selected areas on Admiralty, Naval and other charts. A more detailed source of information for coastal waters is found in tidal stream atlases. It is essential to learn how to read tide tables and the tidal stream information on charts and in tidal atlases before you can take part in planning a passage and plotting a course on a chart.

In simple terms, if you are sailing with the tide your speed over the ground will be your speed through the water plus the rate of the tidal stream. If you have to go the other way it will be your speed through the water less the rate of the tidal stream. (Remember that your log – which is the equivalent in a boat to a speedometer in a car – will register your speed and distance through the water, not over the ground). When the set of the tidal stream is at an angle to the direction in which you are sailing, your actual track as well as your speed over the ground will be affected. So you will have to work out a course to steer which will compensate for the effect of the tide and take you on the required track.

All compass bearings are magnetic, but where is magnetic north this year? The chart will tell you what the current variation is, but charts are orientated to true north (because it remains constant) and so is all the information on them. It is therefore customary to convert compass bearings to true bearings before they are used on a chart, and when writing down or calling out a bearing it must always be made clear whether it is true ('T') or magnetic ('M'). And true bearings worked out on the chart must be converted to magnetic before being passed on to the helmsman who is steering by the compass.

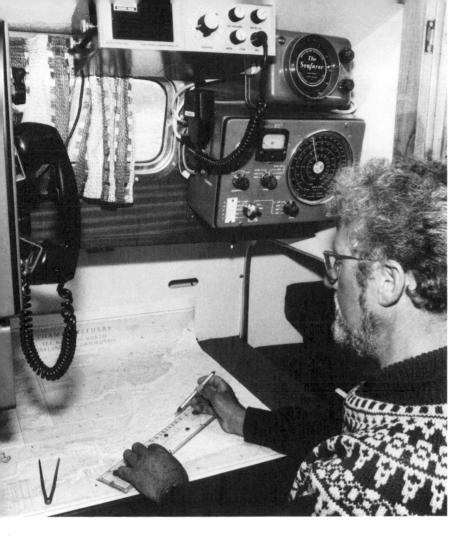

Laying off a bearing on the chart. This boat is equipped with a powerful radio transmitter and receiver for communications world-wide, and a smaller VHF radio telephone (above the window) for short distance coastal communications with shore and other vessels. In the top right hand corner is the echo sounder.

Most charts have one or more compass rose printed on them from which bearings can be taken using a parallel ruler. The outer ring of a compass rose on a chart is graduated in true degrees clockwise round the full 360°. There is usually an inner ring giving magnetic degrees which can be used too if the navigator wants to work in magnetic. But, depending on the age of the chart, the magnetic rose may not be strictly accurate and the variation will have to be allowed for to give absolute accuracy.

Iron, steel and other ferrous metals, and electric circuits and equipment all affect a compass and cause deviation–and there are plenty of things on a boat to do that. However, by the time a boat is ready to sail any compass deviation should have been sorted out and the compass 'corrected'. But you can accidentally make a nonsense compass reading if you put a can of beer, a spanner or portable radio too near it. When using a hand bearing compass the readings are likely to be quite inaccurate if you hold it close to a guardrail or part of the standing rigging which is not marine grade stainless steel. Bearings taken from below through a window because it is wet on deck are often false.

The basic equipment for chart work: chart, sailing directions and/or pilot guide for the area, tidal atlas, pencil, rubber, dividers, parallel rule or other patent plotting device, and nautical almanac—in this case open at the tide tables section.

The chart itself is a fund of information showing navigation marks (buoyage), lights and lighthouses and their characteristics, depth soundings and contour lines in fathoms or metres, tidal eddies, races (turbulent water over shallows or broken ground), the state of the sea bottom and a host of other details. For Admiralty charts there is a publication (Chart No. 5011) explaining all the markings and symbols on their charts, and these are also given in Reed's Almanac. They are well worth serious study at home so that you will recognise them when you see them on a chart, which then becomes very much more meaningful.

The basic tools for chart work are a parallel ruler, a pair of dividers, a sharp pencil and a rubber. The parallel ruler is used to transfer a line on the chart onto the nearest compass rose in order that its bearing may be read, or conversely to transfer a bearing line off the compass rose to somewhere else on the chart. The parallel ruler is awkward to use and liable to slip while being 'walked' across the chart, especially if the boat is rolling or pitching. There are several patent plotting devices on the market which are easier to use, particularly the type where the lines of longitude and latitude on the chart are used and not a rose.

Dividers are for measuring distances in the same way as

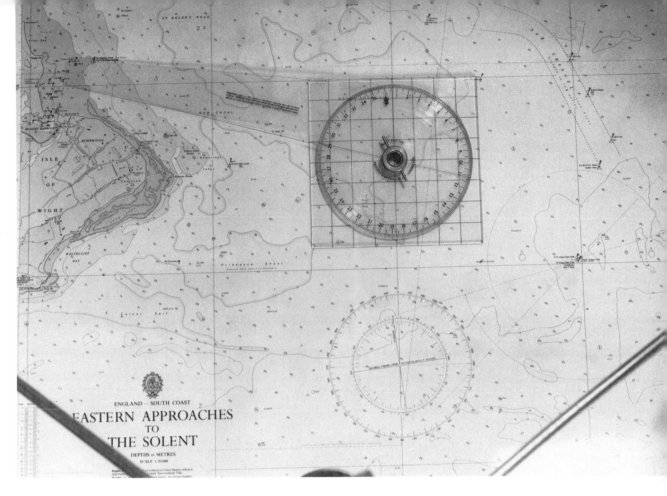

ENGLAND — SOUTH COAST

EASTERN APPROACHES
TO
THE SOLENT

DEPTHS in METRES
SCALE 1:20000

they are on a map, but not off a distance scale. Chart measurements are taken off the vertical latitude scale on the left or right side of the chart, and never off the longitude scales at the top or bottom. The reason for this is that lines of latitude run parallel to each other and are, therefore, the same distance apart all the way round the world, and they do the same on a chart. Lines of longitude are only parallel and equally spaced from each other at the equator. North and south of that line they converge until they meet at the north and south poles. The meridians of longitude are, therefore, a different distance apart in different parts of the world. One minute of longitude is one nautical mile only at the equator, but at the poles it is zero. So the lines of longitude on a chart cannot be used for measuring distance.

Lines of latitude are numbered from 0° at the equator up to 90°N at the north pole and 90°S at the south pole. Each degree is divided into sixty minutes of arc, which is a geometrical unit, and on a chart represents a distance of one nautical mile or 1852 metres. Whatever scale of chart you are looking at the minutes of latitude, each 1/60th of a degree, are shown down the edge of the chart. The distance on any chart between each minute of arc represents 1 nautical mile.

The Hurst Plotter which can be lined up with any line of its grid on, or parallel to, either a longitude or latitude line on the chart. The protractor has been clamped with its 0°–180° axis inclined 6° to the left for a current local variation between true and magnetic of 6° westerly. All bearings read off the Plotter will, therefore, be corrected to magnetic.

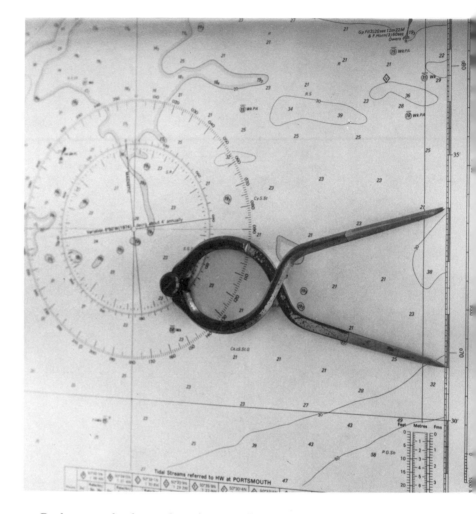

Measuring off 3 nautical miles on the latitude scale on a chart.

Opposite It is fun but wet beating to windward in a Force 6.

On large scale charts there is a parallel scale dividing the minutes of latitude into tenths, therefore each 10th graduation represents 185.2 metres–1/10th of a nautical mile, or near enough 200 yards, and is called a cable. Short distances at sea and in harbour are measured and spoken about in cables or fractions of a cable more often than in yards or metres. The fathom–6 feet–the good old nautical measurement for depth is fast giving way to metres and very soon all charts will have gone metric. The nautical mile and the knot seem to be holding their own against the kilometre.

The use of pencil and rubber are obvious, but pencil lines and markings on charts should be kept to a minimum and be made as lightly as possible compatible with geing able to see them in a dim light at night. Charts are not cheap, and heavy rubbing out shortens their useful life. Ball point pens and indelible pencils must never be allowed near the chart table.

14. Weather forecasts

When sailing nothing is more important than the weather, and no skipper in his right mind will put to sea without a weather forecast. The weather can make all the difference between an enjoyable cruise and a safe arrival, and a taste of purgatory and possible disaster.

Weather forecasts are broadcast by national radio services at frequent intervals, and gale warnings to shipping are broadcast at the earliest opportunity after being received and at the times of news bulletins. Shipping forecasts which are of direct concern to yachtsmen are broadcast in the UK at 0015, 0625, 1355 and 1750 daily on 1500m (200 kHz) and can be received on many portable radios. Coast Radio Stations give bulletins at fixed times on the maritime wavebands and can be received on marine radio telephone equipment and radio receivers which incorporate the marine waveband. Forecasts for inshore waters up to 12 miles from the coast are given immediately after the shipping forecast at 0015.

On land most of the time we listen to weather forecasts with only mild interest and some cynicism. At sea the weather has to be watched and treated very seriously, and shipping forecasts are listened to religiously. Listening, of course, is not enough; the form in which the information is given has to be understood, and then it has to be interpreted and related to the area in which you are sailing. This requires a basic understanding of marine meteorology which, like navigation, can be learnt in the classroom and at home. One does not have to even work with hypothetical situations; the weather is always real even when you are sitting in an armchair at home, and the radio forecasts and weather maps in newspapers and on television are not hypothetical.

Before and during a passage the skipper will listen to all the forecasts so that he can be continually planning ahead to make the best use of the expected wind and weather. You can take your first steps towards understanding the weather by writing down

Opposite above An Air-Sea Rescue helicopter making its run in to a liferaft with the winchman almost walking on the water.
Opposite below The moment of rescue as the helicopter winchman lands on the liferaft with a harness ready to take off the first survivor.

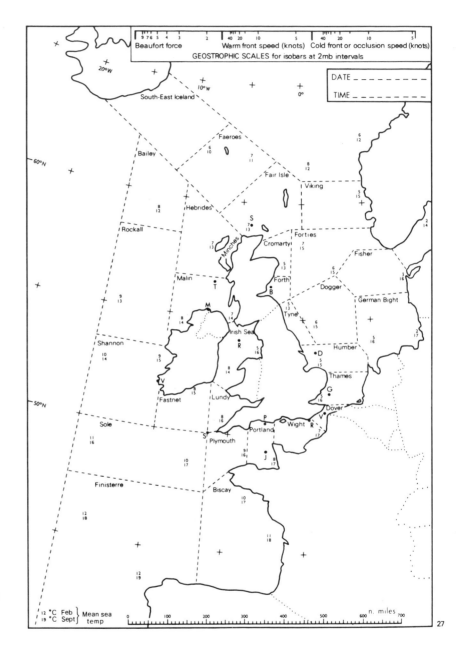

Prepared weather chart for use with the BBC shipping forecasts.

each forecast. They have to be written down because there are far too many details to remember. Bulletins are broadcast at reading not dictation speed, so abbreviations are used. Special printed forms, which include a chart showing the sea areas covered in each forecast, make this and the subsequent interpretation of the information much easier.

Every shipping forecast is in four parts:

1. Gale warnings in force.

2. The general synopsis, which gives the overall picture of the weather in the sea areas covered by the forecast. It tells you where depressions, anticyclones, troughs and fronts were located six hours previously, the speed and direction in which they were moving, and where they are expected to be at the end of the forecast period.

3. The sea area forecast gives the wind, weather and visibility for the following 24 hours in each of a number of specific sea areas. These are read in a fixed sequence. To save time the words 'wind', 'weather' and 'visibility' are left out.

4. Reports from coastal stations. These come at the end of each bulletin and give the local wind direction and force, any significant weather, visibility, barometric pressure in millibars, and whether the barometer is rising, falling or steady. The information in these reports is more up to date than that given in the general synopsis.

There are three categories of gale warning. A 'gale' denotes that the mean wind is expected to increase to force 8 (34 knots) or over, or that gusts of 43 knots or over are expected. A 'severe gale' denotes that the mean wind is expected to increase to force 9 (41 knots) or over, or that gusts of 52 knots or over are expected. A 'storm' denotes that the mean wind is expected to increase to force 10 (48 knots) or over, or that gusts of 61 knots are expected. The yachtsman should consider a forecast of force 6 rising 7 as his gale warning and plan accordingly. In this context 'imminent' means within 6 hours of the issuing of the warning, 'soon' means 6 to 12 hours of the issue, and 'later' is beyond 12 hours of the time of issue.

The general synopsis gives the barometric pressure at the centre of weather systems, and coastal station reports give the recorded local pressure. Generally speaking high pressure is good news and low pressure is bad news. While it can be said that 1020 millibars is a high pressure compared with 1010 millibars, high and low pressures, as far as they affect weather conditions, are relative to the pressure in surrounding areas. It is, therefore, the changes in pressure which are important rather than the pressure itself. The boat's barometer is an excellent weather prophet. The general tendency of the weather is indicated by it rising, falling or remaining steady. What is important to watch is the variation of the needle (changes of pressure) within a period of 3 hours. A drop of 2 to 3 millibars is a sign of worsening weather, 3 to 5 millibars a warning of very bad conditions, and anything over 5 millibars that all hell is about to break loose.

A depression or low is a cyclonic movement in the atmosphere forming a low pressure system bringing bad weather. It can be from 100 to 2,000 miles in diameter and can move in any direction at speeds of up to 60 knots. In a depression the winds always circulate anti-clockwise in the northern hemisphere and clockwise in the southern hemisphere. An anti-cyclone or high is the opposite of a depression and brings fair weather and light winds which circulate clockwise in the northern hemisphere and anticlockwise in the southern hemisphere.

A deepening depression is one where the pressure at the centre is falling and stronger winds and rain can be expected. A vigorous depression means vigorous winds and heavy rain. A complex depression has more than one centre of low pressure and produces complex wind movements. Within any one low pressure system there may be troughs of lower pressure radiating from the centre.

Sometimes a trough will develop into a secondary depression with its own wind circulation and break away as a small rogue weather system. This can happen suddenly and is, therefore, difficult to forecast and so is potentially dangerous. A front is really a trough, and is called a warm front when the air mass changes from cold to warm as the trough passes; a cold front is when the air mass changes from warm to cold.

An anti-cyclone or high is described as building when its pressure is rising, and weakening when its pressure is falling. If its pressure falls rapidly it is said to be collapsing, and so is the good weather. Ridges of high pressure occur between depressions; they are literally ridges with no centres and bring bright periods between dull ones.

The following terms are used in forecasts to describe the speed at which a pressure system moves:
slowly—up to 15 knots; steadily—15 to 25 knots; rather quickly—25 to 35 knots; rapidly—35 to 45 knots; very rapidly—over 45 knots.

Once weather systems are fully understood the information given in forecasts can be used to draw a weather map showing the positions of pressure areas and their speed and direction of movement. Then, by projection, it is possible to predict the direction of the wind at any point along a course for several hours ahead.

15. Passage planning

The annual family holiday cruise is usually a long-planned event; charts and sailing directions are studied as far back as the previous winter, and provisional passage planning done well in advance. The boat is worked up during weekend sailing earlier in the season, any new gear is tested, and all problems are ironed out. The crew for the cruise will probably join the boat for one or two weekends beforehand so that the skipper will know their capabilities and they will know the boat. With any luck they will already be good mates and work as a team.

In crews of four or more there is usually one person who is more interested in navigation than the others and does not mind working below. Hopefully someone else likes cooking, and there will be the tough guy who thinks it is great fun to get soaking wet on a pitching foredeck. The who-does-what-job problem is often solved by the different temperaments of the individuals who make up the team.

Even so, on a cruise lasting more than a few days and if there is any night sailing, everybody has to do all of the jobs some of the time otherwise nobody would get any rest. Even the skipper has to sleep while the boat is sailing, and so does the navigator.

Steering a boat requires a lot of concentration, and a one-hour 'trick' on the helm is some people's limit; two hours is the norm. So everybody has to take his or her turn whatever other jobs they do. At night there will probably be only two people on watch at a time—one on the helm, the other keeping a look out, trimming the sails, plotting the course, keeping the log and making the essential hot drinks at frequent intervals.

The necessity of job sharing and team work on a cruise should ensure that you get plenty of practical experience right from the start. But there is the possibility—if your first cruise is with experienced friends and they are in a hurry to get on and make good mileage—that they will treat you more as a passenger than as a full crew member.

Before starting off on a day's sail the family do their passage planning with chart and tidal atlas.

It might be better to get your initial experience on a coastal cruising course with a crew of beginners like yourself and a qualified instructor as skipper. You will then have to share all the jobs equally. Such a cruise may not be quite as enjoyable socially as sailing with friends, but you will learn more. One advantage of sailing with a professional instructor is that nothing essential will be omitted, particularly the all-important passage planning. On a cruising course you will be made to do it together on board before you sail, and it will have to be up-dated daily.

Having decided on a destination, intended course lines are plotted on the chart and also alternative courses which may have to be taken if the original course is abandoned due to adverse weather or for any other reason. A straight line from point of departure to destination is very rarely the course which can be sailed. The intended course will be that which is found to be the most favourable after taking into account the following factors:

The positions of hazards and dangers shown on the chart and listed in the pilot book or sailing directions.

The predicted states of tides and their rate and set during the length of the passage which are worked out from tide tables in the nautical almanac and the tidal atlas.

The wind strength and direction, and any expected changes in them as predicted on the weather chart and by the latest forecast.

There is a limit to the amount of passage planning that you can do because you do not know in advance how fast you are going to go. Your speed will depend on the wind strength and direction, and unless that comes exactly as forecast any plan will have to be modified as you go along.

The tidal streams will affect both the track of the boat over the ground and the duration of the passage, as will also the strength and direction of the wind. Then there is the question of leeway which only the skipper, who knows the perfromance of his boat, will be able to estimate. But whatever leeway the boat does make it will be greater along any section of the course when she is close hauled. A safe and favourable course can only be plotted after taking all the natural elements into account and estimating their effects on the boat's course and speed.

There may be several other factors to be considered, notably the estimated time of arrival at your destination. The time of departure or the time spent at sea may have to be adjusted to ensure sufficient height of tide to allow for a safe approach and entry into harbour.

In many cases it is better to work back from your destination allowing for the slowest speed you can safely estimate. If it is essential to get somewhere within two hours of high water and you can assume that you will average at least 2 knots, you will at least know the latest time for departure. Then if you do go faster than expected you can always sail around for an hour or so at the other end, whereas if you arrive too late it may mean a wait at sea for perhaps 8 hours. Tide races, which are often found in narrow straits between an island and the mainland and off prominent headlands, are best negotiated at slack water. When wind is against tide they might be dangerous, so a course will have to be set to keep well clear of them.

The tidal stream is normally weaker near the coast and it often turns earlier than the main stream, so it might be helpful to plan a course which runs offshore during a fair tide and then closes the land to make better way against a weaker foul tide which will turn in your favour before the main stream does. The state of the tide determines the depth of water over rocks and shoal areas which may be safe to cross at high water, but which become hazards to be avoided at low water.

If making for an anchorage it will have to be one which can be entered and which offers shelter in the prevailing wind and tide conditions and, in case they change on the way, an alternative must be planned for. There are endless computations which can be worked out in advance, and the time spent on passage planning, and the amount of detail that is gone into, will depend on the skipper and his judgment of how difficult the passage is going to be.

The object of the exercise is to cut down the amount of chart work which has to be done at sea and to collate all the information on navigation aids, tides, harbours, shelters, etc. so that it is instantly available for quick reference while under way.

16. Liferaftsmanship

The inflatable liferaft is the ultimate item of safety equipment which should be carried by any boat going far offshore or making extended passages. It is a very expensive piece of equipment to buy and never use, and good seamanship should ensure that you never do have to use it; but if and when it should suddenly be your only means of staying alive . . . . then what price your life and the lives of your family or friends?

If you are a fair weather sailor and cruise in an estuary or near the coast during the season, always within sight of other boats and ships, then an inflatable dinghy, partially inflated on deck and equipped with at least a pair of oars, is quite sufficient. But if you sail off some of the less popular coastlines, away from shipping lanes, in areas where winds and strong currents can take you far out to sea, especially in bad and cold weather, then an open dinghy would not be enough. You might not sink, but you could die of exposure before you were found. For that once-a-year holiday cruise to sea you can hire a liferaft by the week.

It is possible for a liferaft to malfunction, but if it does it will be too late to complain to the manufacturer. The only safeguard is to have it serviced before the start of every season.

The liferaft, whether in a flat or round canister, must be stowed on deck, absolutely never below, and should sit on chocks or a cradle designed for the purpose. It should be held securely against every possible motion of the boat with efficient quick-release fastenings. Rot-proof webbing straps with an instant release mechanism, such as Senhouse slips, are the very best method. Shock cords should not be used as they are not strong enough, they can chafe and perish and the hooks can get snarled at a time when seconds are precious. Rope lashings with slip knots are dangerous. Knots have a habit of jamming, especially when tied by inexperienced hands. Then the ropes will have to be cut with a knife—if a knife can be found in a hurry. Of course every sailor should carry one, but does he?

The advantage of a valise type liferaft, apart from being cheaper than one in a canister, is that it can be stowed in a cockpit locker out of the way. But it is most important that the static line is secured to a ring or other fixed point inside the locker otherwise it would be all too likely, in the panic of the moment, that the valise would be taken out of the locker and thrown overboard, static line and all, to float away unopened.

The soft valise type pack must not be stowed deep in the bowels of the boat. Ideally it should be stowed in a locker opening directly into the cockpit and containing the liferaft only. The risk with the valise is that someone might throw it in the sea without first attaching the painter to the boat. If kept in a special locker with access to the cockpit then the painter can be permanently secured.

One of the most important points of liferaft stowage is the securing of the painter. It must always remain very securely fastened to a strong part on the boat. Only a short length protrudes from the canister, but a longer length can be pulled out to reach the best strong point, but not more of the painter than is waterproofed otherwise it will act as a wick and allow water into the canister or valise. Better to lengthen it with another piece of rope. The painter does three jobs: it keeps the liferaft in its canister attached to the boat after it has been thrown overboard; it actuates the automatic inflation; and it keeps the inflated liferaft from drifting or blowing away. If the painter is not secured to the boat the canister will float away unopened when it is thrown overboard. So do not rely on remembering to tie it to something at the last moment.

Left Unless the boat is moving fast, or there is a strong sea running, the static line of a life-raft may not pull all the way out of its canister to activate the CO_2 inflation system. It should then be pulled out by hand and given a sharp tug.

Right There is always a fair chance that a liferaft will inflate upside down, or will be blown or tossed upside down in a heavy sea. Then a strong crew member will have to go overboard first and climb up onto its bottom to right it.

Once the canister is in the water the automatic inflation is actuated by a sharp tug on the painter. If it is blown downwind this will probably happen when it gets to the end of its length of painter – about 25 ft (8 m). But if it is thrown over the weather side it may stay close to the boat, in which case the full length of the painter will have to be pulled out by hand and finally given a good tug.

If the sea is not too rough, and if the boat is not rolling too much, it may be possible to haul the liferaft in close alongside and step or drop over the side and go straight in through the opening in the canopy. That is the best way because nobody gets wet. If the opening is not facing the side of the boat it is still possible to get in dry-shod by falling spread-eagle onto the canopy, which will partially collapse under the weight and form a sort of hammock, out of which you can roll into the opening, but this is not recommended in rough seas.

There could be a situation where the strength of the wind keeps the liferaft streaming out taut on the end of its painter, or where the motion of the boat and the sea make it impossible or dangerous to keep the liferaft alongside. In those circumstances there is no alternative but to swim out to it holding onto the painter. The safest way is for each member of the crew to have his

It looks unkind, but it is very
effective and is the approved
way of getting an exhausted or
unconscious man into a liferaft.

Above A waterproof pack of red parachute distress signals. Do you know where they are stowed on the boat?
Below The complete answer to keeping distress signals dry and ready to hand. Should you have to abandon ship this canister goes with you into the liferaft.

safety line hooked onto the painter. It is then possible to swim with both arms, or to go hand-over-hand along the painter with no fear of being swept away.

Whichever method of embarking is used, it is not a question of women and children first—the strongest and most resourceful member of the crew should be the first to go into the liferaft. Liferafts are very difficult to get into from the water, and if crew have to go out along the painter it is necessary that the first out is the strongest so that he can help his weaker, or any sick or injured, mates to get in.

Lifejackets need to be half deflated before attempting to climb up over the two buoyancy tubes otherwise they get in the way. To get a very heavy or an unconscious person into the liferaft leave his lifejacket inflated, turn him with his back to the entrance, grasp him firmly by the shoulders and push his head under the water. His buoyancy will immediately be increased and he will pop up like a cork. As he comes up he can be heaved inboard while his momentum is still reducing his weight. It sounds drastic, but it works.

When everyone is in the liferaft it is cast off by cutting the painter; there is a knife for this purpose in a pocket inside the raft. The first job when everybody is in the liferaft is to bale out any water that has got in during boarding. If a sea is running, if there is spray flying or a cold wind blowing, the entrance must be closed. Any injured crew must be kept as warm as possible with dry clothing, if available, otherwise by hugging. If the sea is cold then the floor of the liferaft will be equally cold—unless it is the type which can be inflated.

It is impossible to navigate a liferaft; it can only drift with wind and tide. If a MAYDAY signal was sent before the boat was abandoned, or if distress signals were sent up, it is necessary to remain near your last reported position. The drogue sea anchor attached to the liferaft will reduce the drift and also tend to keep the vulnerable entrance away from the weather and ease the motion of the raft.

But if your last position cannot be known to anyone, and if you are very certain that a drift downwind will take you nearer to land or a regular shipping lane for rescue, then the drogue can be taken in. When 'sailing' downwind a slight amount of steerage might be managed by using the paddles supplied.

It is essential that watches are kept, both against the risk of being run down and in order to watch for and signal to the rescue services. Distress signals should be used sparingly, and in haze or fog it will be necessary to wait for clearer visibility before using them. Parachute flares are best at night and when far from land or shipping during the day. Hand flares should be used (but kept at arm's length from the raft) when near other vessels or the shore, and to give your location to rescue boats when you hear or see one coming, and to guide an air-sea rescue helicopter at night. During the day smoke signals are best for giving your position to an aircraft, although if it is flying high or wide a parachute flare can be used to alert it. The same advice applies if distress signals are used from a boat in distress which has not been abandoned.

In case of leaks or damage there is a repair kit with instructions provided in the raft. The rescue beacon on the top of the canopy is operated by a sea-activated battery dangling in the water. To save power the battery should be pulled inboard during the day. The smell and the motion of a liferaft are very sickmaking, and even those who are never seasick on a boat are likely to succumb. If there is any thought that the crew may have to abandon ship everyone on board should take a seasick pill just in case, and a supply should also be taken into the liferaft.

A liferaft will only save you from drowning and give you protection from windchill and continuous saturating spray. But after that your survival, if rescue is delayed too long, will depend on what you have taken into the raft with you. The manufacturers sell basic survival packs and deep sea packs which conform to RORC (Royal Ocean Racing Club) rules and which can be packed in with your liferaft. Which pack you select will depend on the range of your sailing.

When passage making in bad weather keep emergency supplies in a sailbag or other soft container where it can be quickly found, picked up and taken into the raft. It should contain dry clothes (warm or lightweight, according to the season and latitudes), concentrated food (with a bit of flavour for morale), and also for morale cigarettes and matches. Everything should be waterproofed in plastic bags. A waterproof torch with spare batteries and extra distress signals, including smoke, are some of the obvious contents.

All the other basic needs should already be in the manufacturer's survival pack in the liferaft, but check their list. If there is time take a plastic can of water too. There should be tins of water in the raft, but the quantity is minimal and you can live for at least 10 days on water without food. Plain biscuits may be dull to eat, but nibbled frequently they help to keep seasickness at bay.

Wet clothes in cold weather, especially at night, can cause hypothermia which, together with continual vomiting causing dehydration, can be fatal. Sick crew should be given the driest clothes. Constipation and difficulty in urinating are normal and no cause for alarm.

Do you know how to use the distress signals on board? Could you activate them by feel only in the dark?

17. Man overboard

Before going very far with a new or novice crew a skipper should make everyone on board practise man overboard drill. 'Gybe at once' is the immediate reaction of most yachtsmen because it is the drill which has been taught for many generations, but it is seldom taught nowadays. The manoeuvre which is more approved now is to reach out, tack, and reach back. This is a safety drill which all crew members need to practise several times from each point of sailing before settling down to a cruise at sea.

If you fall overboard it is to be hoped that the skipper knows what to do and how to do it, but what if he should fall over and you, the novice, have to rescue him? You will be in the same situation as the wife who has never been allowed to take charge of the boat and then her husband falls overboard. The following drill is one which the beginner with only a little sailing experience should be able to handle.

The first person to see someone fall overboard shouts loudly 'man overboard' and immediately throws a lifebuoy to him. If it goes wide he quickly throws a second one – there should be two on the pushpit. If the person who saw the victim go over is not in the cockpit the helmsman will have to do the throwing – which is another reason for a loud shout.

Providing he is not left alone on board, the person who raised the alarm should do nothing but keep his eyes on the victim and continuously inform the helmsman where he is relative to the boat. Otherwise he will have to sail the boat and try to watch the victim at the same time; it will require a very cool head not to get disorientated by trying to look two ways at once.

The quickest and often the safest action is to start the engine and motor back with the sails free. But if there is a strong wind blowing which might take charge of the boat even when the sails are free, or if visibility is bad, the helmsman can motor-sail, driving the boat onto a beam reach (90° to the wind) and, after going on that tack for a short distance, go about and come back on a

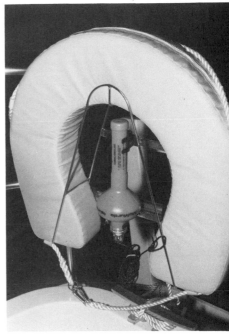

MAN OVERBOARD

Left It can happen in the nicest weather if you do not keep one hand for the boat.
Above Lifebuoy and flashing light ready for use on an instant release bracket on the pushpit. The light floats and switches itself on as soon as it is turned the right way up.

The sea is calm, the light fairly good, and the boat is near. The man overboard would be a much more indistinct target in a rough sea and/or poor visibility.

reciprocal beam reach. This should bring the boat near the victim; it is then turned into the wind to approach him. The engine must be put in neutral as the boat comes alongside the victim.

By making that manoeuvre there is no risk of a gybe which the beginner might not be able to manage or which, in strong wind conditions, might get out of control, cause damage and delay the whole operation. It also has the advantage that if smartly executed it will automatically bring the boat back fairly close to the point from which it started, which is essential when visibility is poor. If the engine fails to start immediately the same manoeuvre is used under sail only to get back to the man in the water.

If the engine is switched on it must be kept in neutral until a check has been made that there are no sheets hanging overboard. If you are not very careful it is possible to end up with a jib sheet round the propeller and bar taut so that the engine cannot be used and neither can the headsail. If there is enough wind for someone to fall overboard there is enough wind to sail the boat; if not, falling overboard is not so serious except at night. An engine running in neutral is a useful stand-by to give a nudge ahead or to take way off the boat on reaching the victim.

When there is a steep sea running or in poor visibility it helps to lay a trail to follow back. Anything that floats—empty beer cans, cushions, even torn up charts—can be used. Newspaper and lavatory paper sink almost immediately, so are useless.

Meanwhile the victim should have inflated his life jacket and be

One way of getting a man up over the topsides is to use the topping lift – as in this case, or one of the halyards as a hoist.

holding one arm out of the water to make himself more visible. If he has managed to reach the lifebuoy he should get into it. It will give him extra buoyancy and keep him higher in the water. A shirt, scarf or cap waved above his head will increase his chances of being seen, and at night or if it is getting dark he can detach the light from his lifejacket or the one from the lifebuoy and hold it above his head like the Statue of Liberty.

Most people steer a boat sitting on the windward side, from which position they can see almost right ahead on the weather side. But they have a blind area through the bow of the boat and on the lee side. If the approach is made with the man in the water on the windward side of the boat the helmsman can watch him all the time. If the approach is made up wind of the victim the helmsman will lose sight of him under the lee bow, and if he happens to get disorientated at that particular time he may run the victim down. On the other hand it is easier to lift a man over the lee side of a boat, and if the sails were to be sheeted in tight the boat might heel sufficiently for the victim to 'swim' back on board.

Getting hold of the victim and getting him back on board, especially in a heavy sea, can be far harder than bringing the boat back to him. A boat hook offered for him to grab can become an offensive weapon if the boat is wallowing and he is bobbing about. But if he is unconscious it may be necessary to get the hook onto a strap of his lifejacket or some loose part of his clothing to bring him alongside.

Left This picture illustrates how difficult it is to haul one's self up over even the lowest part of a boat's topsides, especially aft where your legs float under the stern. The crewman has got a bowline around the victim and is about to secure it inboard to keep him safely attached to the boat.

Right Then he gets a loop of a sheet overboard to give the victim a strop to support his feet.

If you are alone on board there is a danger of getting into the situation where you are hanging onto the man in the water but unable to lift him up. It is stalemate and sooner or later you will have to let go and lose him. Always get a rope ready with a bowline on the end while manoeuvring for the pick-up, and get the loop over the victim's head and under his arms. Then with the other end tied to the boat he is secured alongside and will not become totally exhausted while hanging on, nor will he drift away. You now have a little time to think how best to get him back on board.

That will not be easy. He may be exhausted and unable to help himself. With his waterlogged clothes he will be very heavy, and he is unlikely to have the strength to pull himself up over the topsides even with you helping. If he can get the bowline round his backside and sit, kneel or stand in it, it may be possible to use a sheet winch to get him up high enough to scramble inboard. This is a useful method when there is only one person on board, particularly a not so strong wife or youngster. But the victim has to be in a state to collaborate.

If the boat is substantially rigged, the mainsheet can be shackled, hooked or tied to the becket of his lifejacket, or a bowline in the sheet can be put under his arms and the boom, supported by the topping lift, used like the gantry of a crane to hoist

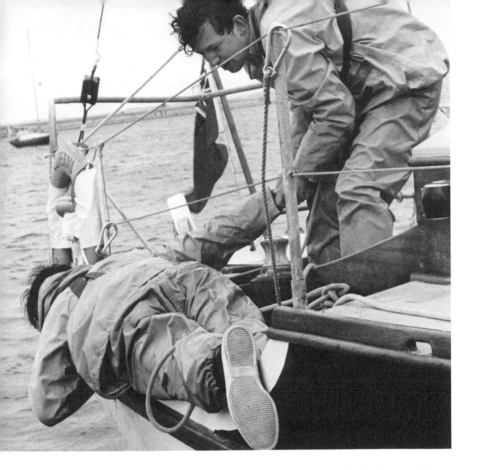

Finally the victim is got inboard. All very undignified and taking quite a lot of effort –but it was only in harbour. Imagine the same situation in heavy sea with the boat rolling.

him inboard. A very cruel last resort technique in bad conditions is to get the mainsheet attached to the victim and then do a violent gybe all standing. He will land in the cockpit like a fish on the end of a line, bruised if not broken.

One method of recovery which is worth practising is using the inflatable dinghy; it must be already on deck partially inflated. During the manoeuvring back to the victim the inflatable is tipped over the side of the boat with its painter secured a little forward of the beam. It will then ride alongside nose up, and it should be easy to steer the boat close enough for the person in the water to grab hold of some part of such a large soft object. What-ever part he gets hold of, the deflated bow section will make it easy for him to scramble or roll into it.

If he is unconscious or exhausted a member of the crew, with a lifeline attached to him, can get down into the inflatable where he will be in a safe position level with the water to grab hold of the victim and haul him in. There he can rest safely before the exertion of getting back on board, which will be much easier from the level of the inflatable on top of the water than from in the water.

Unfortunately it is not a method which can be used in heavy seas when the inflatable could be tossed back on board or its painter torn loose.

Beaufort Scale of Wind Speed

Beaufort No.	Seaman's description of wind	Terms used in U.S. Weather Bureau forecasts	Wind Speed in knots	Approximate pressure in lb per ft^2	Description of sea
0	Calm	Light	Less than 1	Less than 0.01	Sea like a mirror.
1	Light air	Light	1–3	0.01–0.06	Ripples, no foam crests.
2	Light breeze	Light	4–6	0.06–0.2	Small wavelets, crests have a glassy appearance and do not break.
3	Gentle breeze	Gentle	7–10	0.2–0.4	Large wavelets, crests begin to break. Perhaps scattered white caps.
4	Moderate breeze	Moderate	11–16	0.4–1.0	Small waves becoming longer. Fairly frequent white caps.
5	Fresh breeze	Fresh	17–21	1.0–2.0	Moderate waves, taking a more pronounced long form. Many white caps, some spray.
6	Strong breeze	Strong	22–27	2.0–3.0	Large waves begin to form. Extensive white caps everywhere, some spray.
7	Moderate gale (high wind)	Strong	28–33	3.0–4.0	Sea heaps up and white foam from breaking waves begins to be blown in well-marked streaks along the direction of the wind.

8	Fresh gale	Gale	34–40	4.0–6.0	Moderately high waves of greater length. Edges of crests break into spindrift. The foam is blown in well-marked streaks along the direction of the wind.
9	Strong gale	Gale	41–47	6.0–9.0	High waves. Dense streaks of foam along the direction of the wind. Spray may affect visibility. Sea begins to roll.
10	Whole gale (heavy gale)	Whole gale	48–55	9.0–12.0	Very high waves with long overhanging crests. Surface of the sea takes on a white appearance. Rolling of the sea becomes heavy and shock-like. Visibility is affected.
11	Storm	Whole gale	56–65	12.0–16.0	Exceptionally high waves. Sea is completely covered with long white patches of foam. Visibility is affected. Small- and medium-sized ships are lost to view for long periods.
12	Hurricane	Hurricane	Above 65	Above 16.0	Air is filled with foam and spray. Sea completely white with driving spray. Visibility very seriously affected.

Well-marked streaks along the direction of the wind – rising force 7.

The Beaufort scale of wind force can be judged on land by the following criteria:

Force 0 – Smoke rises vertically.

Force 1 – Smoke drifts, showing wind direction.

Force 2 – Start to feel wind on the face, leaves rustle, flags flap and wind vanes move.

Force 3 – Leaves and light rubbish in continual movement. Flags fly fully extended.

Force 4 – Leaves and dust are raised and small branches sway.

Force 5 – Wavelets with crests on lakes and large ponds. Small trees start to sway.

Force 6 – Umbrellas difficult to hold, telephone cables whistle, large branches swing.

Force 7 – Effort needed to walk against the wind, complete trees sway.

Force 8 – Have to battle against the wind when walking, and twigs are broken off trees.

Glossary

ABACK A sail which has filled on the wrong side so that the boat tends to be blown to leeward or backwards. When done purposely the sails are 'laid aback', and 'taken aback' when it is accidental.

ABAFT Behind. Aft of amidships.

ABOUT To go about is to tack. To be about is to have completed a tack.

ACCIDENTAL GYBE When the boat is running and the wind gets on the same quarter as the mainsail is set and blows it across to the other side of the boat unexpectedly and, perhaps, violently.

AFT The area towards the stern. Back end of.

ALL STANDING All sails up. Mostly used when referring to an accidental gybe as 'gybing all standing'.

AMIDSHIPS The middle line of a boat either fore and aft or athwartships. The middle part of a boat.

ANGLE OF HEEL The angle at which a boat leans over on one side.

APPARENT WIND The true wind plus the wind created by the boat's forward movement, or the true wind less the speed of the boat when the wind is coming from behind. Except when running, the apparent wind is ahead of the true wind.

ASTERN In reverse. Behind the vessel.

ATHWART, ATHWARTSHIPS Anything at right angles to the boat's fore and aft line.

BACKSTAY The stay which supports the mast from behind to prevent it from bending or falling forwards. There may be one or two backstays.

BATTENS Wood, metal or plastic slats slid into pockets along the leech of a sail to keep it flat.

BATTEN DOWN To close or shut down hatches, etc.

BEAM The width of a boat at her widest point. 'On the beam' is at right angles to the boat's fore and aft line.

BEAM REACH A point of sailing with the wind on the beam.

BEAR AWAY Turn a boat away from the wind.

BEAT A course sailed close to the wind. Beating is sailing near to the wind, close hauled, usually not nearer than 45°.

BELAY Make fast a rope round a cleat or other fixed object.

BEND A knot formed to be easily cast off. To tie or make fast.

BERMUDAN RIG A rig which has a tall triangular mainsail with its luff attached to the mast.

BIGHT A bend or loop in a wire or rope.

BILGE That part of a boat where hull and keel meet. Also commonly used to describe the empty spaces under the cockpit and cabin soles which are called 'the bilges'.

BILGE KEELER A boat with twin keels.

BLOCK A wood, metal or plastic casing with one or more pulley wheels (sheaves) inside it, round which wire or rope runs to gain a mechanical advantage, or to lead a rope off at an angle. A snatch block opens to allow the wire or rope to be taken over the pulley without having to thread (reeve) it through.

BOLLARD A fixed solid object round which mooring lines can be looped or belayed. On board they are usually arranged in pairs to take a figure-of-eight, or in the form of a single vertical timber or metal stump also called a sampson post.

BOOM The spar of wood or metal to which the foot of a sail is attached. Most often refers to the main boom which controls the mainsail. Can be any spar rigged overboard to act as a gantry.

BOW The stem, front, forward part of a boat. The 'sharp end'.

BOW ROLLER Also stem head roller. Takes the anchor rope or chain and, by revolving like a pulley wheel, allows it to run out or be hauled in without friction.

BOWSPRIT A spar rigged or fixed projecting forward of the bows to which one or more headsails are attached by their tacks.

BREAST ROPE A mooring line led at right angles from the boat to the shore or another boat.

BRIGANTINE A two-masted boat schooner rigged on the mainmast but with square sails on the foremast.

BROACH To slew round in a bad sea when running, with the risk of the wind getting behind the sails and pressing the boat over.

BROAD REACH A point of sailing with the wind coming from over one quarter.

BUOY Anchored floating mark for navigation. Also that to which a boat can be moored, or which can be picked up with its length of chain or rope and made fast on board. A Dan buoy has a spar or pole through it with a flag or other mark on top and is used as a racing marker or is attached to a lifebuoy to mark the position of a man overboard.

BUOYAGE The system of buoys or navigational marks laid to mark fairways, channels, entrances, hazards.

BURGEE A triangular flag indicating membership of a club, association or other body. May also be a house or owner's personal pennant.

CENTRE OF EFFORT The point at which the force of the wind is presumed to act on the sails for the purpose of making calculations.

CENTRE OF LATERAL RESISTANCE The point about which a boat pivots, being the point at which the forces on the sails and superstructure balance the resistance of the hull/keel in the water.

CLEAT A wood or metal fitting with two 'horns' round which a chain or rope can be belayed.

CLEW The corner of a sail to which sheets are attached, or the corner which is attached to the outboard end of a boom.

CLOSE HAULED Sailing as close to the wind as possible.

CLOSE REACH Point of sailing with the wind just ahead of the beam.

CLOSE TACKING Making a number of short tacks in succession. Tacking in zig-zag fashion within a narrow channel, fairway or between hazards or obstructions.

COACHROOF The raised roof of a cabin inboard of a boat's sides.

COAMING The raised side of a cockpit, or wall round a hatch or well.

COCKPIT The after area or sunken deck of a boat where the helmsman sits.

CRINGLES Rope or metal rings or 'thimbles' sewn or riveted into the corners of sails to take ropes or shackles for sheets or reef lines.

CURRENT A flow of water in one direction. May be tidal or from other causes.

CUTTER A single-masted boat with two headsails.

DEAD RECKONING The position of a boat calculated from the course steered, her speed through the water and elapsed time. It is very much an estimated position which must then take into account the effects of wind and tide.

DEVIATION The amount by which the reading on the compass differs from the position of magnetic north. Deviation is caused by non ferrous metal objects and by magnetic fields created by electrical and electronic installations on a boat.

DISPLACEMENT The weight of a boat, which is equal to the weight of the water which she displaces when afloat.

DODGER Canvas screen round a cockpit to protect the crew from spray.

DOWNHAUL A rope or tackle fitted to haul down a sail or spar, usually to haul the luff down taut.

DOWN WIND Sailing, motoring or drifting with the wind behind the boat. Also refers to the direction to leeward.

DRAFT, DRAUGHT The depth to which a boat sits in the water. The distance between the waterline and the lowest part of the hull or keel. Can also be the depth of curvature in the cross section of a sail. A shoal draft boat is one which has small enough draft to cross shallower water than a deep draft or deep keel boat.

DRAG When a boat moves because her anchor is not holding she drags her anchor. Drag is used to describe the effect of friction between a boat and the water. A stationary propeller on a sailing boat causes drag.

DRAW When a sail fills with wind it is said to draw. A boat draws so many feet draft.

DRIFT The movement of a tidal stream measured in knots. To move with a stream or current, or to be blown along by the wind as opposed to actually sailing.

DROGUE A device used to slow down the movement of a boat. Usually an open-ended cone shaped canvas 'bucket' trailed astern. Sometimes used when a boat is running before a heavy following sea. The appropriate conditions for the use of a drogue depend very much on the characteristics of a boat and is a somewhat controversial subject.

EBB TIDE A falling tide. In a river or estuary the ebb runs out towards the sea. Ebb is the opposite of flood.

ENSIGN The marine equivalent of a national flag. Always flown at or near the stern of a boat.

ESTIMATED POSITION The position of a boat calculated from dead reckoning plus allowances for tidal drift and leeway. See 'dead reckoning'.

EVEN KEEL A boat on an even keel sits upright.

EYE OF THE WIND The direction from which the

true wind is blowing. When a boat tacks she has to turn through the eye of the wind.

FAIRLEAD A fitting with two inward curving 'horns' or a ring through which wires or ropes are led so that they maintain position or direction without slipping or chafing.

FAIRWAY The navigable part of any stretch of water. Usually refers to a buoyed channel. Also has certain legal connotations similar to a public highway.

FALL The part of a rope on which one hauls.

FATHOM The nautical measurement of 6 ft (1·82 m).

FENDER A soft object hung over the side of a boat to act as a buffer to protect the topsides from damage when alongside.

FILL Sails 'fill' with wind.

FIN KEEL One which protrudes below the hull as a separate shape and does not run the length of the hull.

FINE ON Very near to. Fine on the port or starboard bow would be slightly off dead ahead.

FIX The position of a boat determined by the intersection of two or more compass bearings taken on sighted objects or radio signals.

FLAKE To lay a rope or chain down in flat layers so that it is ready to run.

FLOOD TIDE A rising or incoming tide.

FLUKE The pointed arm(s) of an anchor. The part which digs in. A light wind of variable strength and duration is said to be fluky.

FOLLOWING SEA A sea with waves moving in the same direction as the boat.

FOOT The bottom edge of a sail, or the bottom end of anything such as the foot of a mast.

FORE A prefix applied to anything which is on or near the front part of a boat, viz. foredeck hand, foremast, forestay.

FORE AND AFT Lengthwise of the boat, from stem to stern.

FOREDECK That part of the deck in front of the foremast.

FORESAIL On a cutter, sloop, ketch or yawl is the sail(s) forward of the mainmast.

FOUL Foul ground is an anchorage with underwater obstructions in which an anchor can become entangled. A foul wind is one coming from the direction you want to go. A foul tide is one running against you.

FREEBOARD The height of the hull above the waterline. Also called the topsides.

FURL To roll, fold or gather up a sail, flag or other fabric.

GAFF The spar to which the head of a sail is attached. Gaff rigged describes a boat with a quadrilateral fore and aft sail attached to a gaff.

GALLOWS A fixture on which the end of the boom is supported when the sail has been lowered. Not common on modern boats.

GENOA A large headsail which extends aft of the mast.

GIMBALS A mechanism by which an object (e.g. cooker or compass) is suspended so that it pivots either one or two ways to remain horizontal when a boat heels or pitches.

GOOSENECK A universal coupling between the boom and the mast.

GOOSEWING An arrangement of the mainsail set on one side of the boat and the headsail on the other when running before the wind.

GUARDRAILS Safety rails or life lines supported by stanchions which run round a boat to prevent crew from falling overboard.

GYBE To change tack by bringing the stern of the boat through the wind. The opposite manoeuvre to tacking, when the head goes through the wind.

HALYARDS Wires or ropes used to haul things up.

HANK A form of shackle for attaching the luff of a sail to a stay.

HARDEN IN To trim a sail in tighter, flatter.

HAWSE PIPE The hole or pipe through which the anchor chain or rope runs through the deck to the anchor locker.

HEAD Top corner of a triangular sail. The bow of a boat. 'The heads' is also the nautical term for a sea lavatory.

HEADSAIL Any sail set forward of the mainmast or foremast.

HEAD TO WIND When a boat is pointing directly into the wind.

HEEL To lie over at an angle under the pressure of wind in the sails.

HELM The tiller or wheel used to steer a boat by turning the rudder. To steer a boat. Helmsman is the man who steers.

HORSE A transverse bar or track on which a traveller attached to the lower block of a mainsheet can move from side to side.

HULL The main body or shell of a boat. In some contexts it refers to the underwater shape of a boat.

INBOARD Within the boat. A spar or clew of a sail is brought inboard. An inboard engine is mounted inside a boat, whereas an outboard engine is hung on the transom.

INFLATABLE The common name for a tender which is inflated for use, and deflated for stowing. Made of neoprene or similar synthetic rubber-coated fabric.

INSHORE The waters near the shore. An inshore passage would be made within sight of the coast. Offshore would normally mean out of sight of land. There is no precise definition of either word.

ISOBAR A line which joins together areas of equal barometric pressure on a weather map.

ISOTHERM A line which joins together areas of equal temperature.

JAWS The half round fitting at the end of a gaff which fits either side of the mast.

JIB The triangular sail which is foremost when there is more than one headsail, commonly the single headsail of a boat with only two sails.

JURY RIG A makeshift rig erected after a dismasting, or a temporary rudder arrangement.

KEDGE A second, lighter anchor than the main or bow anchor. Used in tandem with the main anchor to reduce the swing of a boat, or for extra holding power. To kedge is to take the lighter anchor off in a tender, drop it overboard, and then haul on its cable to move the boat.

KEEL The backbone of a boat to which sides, stem and transom are attached. Also refers to the ballast keel hung below the boat, which may be either straight and the length of the boat, or a short fin, to provide directional and righting stability.

KETCH A two-masted boat with the shorter (mizzen) mast stepped forward of the rudder post.

KICKING STRAP Sometimes called a vang. A rope or tackle from the foot of the mast or the deck to the underside of the boom to hold it down when the sail fills on a run or broad reach when it tends to lift.

KNOT A speed measurement equal to one nautical mile per hour.

LANDFALL Approaching the land after a relatively long passage, especially out of sight of land. To make a good landfall is to make an accurate one.

LATITUDE Meridians, lines of distance north or south of the equator measured in degrees (90° north and 90° south) which are sub-divided into minutes and seconds.

LEAD A block or eye through which a rope is passed to lead it in a required direction. The weight on the end of a marked line for taking depth soundings.

LEADING MARK A mark or object used as a navigational guide into port, fairway, anchorage, etc. Two such marks in transit indicate the safe line of approach, or departure if viewed astern.

LEE Sheltered from the wind. The lee or leeside of a boat is the one downwind, opposite to the windward or weather side.

LEE HELM A boat's tendency to turn her head downwind. Putting the helm/tiller down towards the lee has the effect of turning the boat's head back into the wind.

LEE SHORE A shore to leeward or downwind of a boat onto which she would be blown if she could not sail or motor off. A boat beating gradually to windward to clear a lee shore is said to be 'clawing off', a potentially dangerous situation when there is no room to tack/manoeuvre.

LEEWAY The angle between the fore and aft line of a boat, and the direction in which the hull is moving under the pressure of the wind. The distance she is driven downwind from her intended course.

LET FLY Let a sheet go suddenly, especially to spill wind from the sail.

LIFEBUOY Buoyant ring or horseshoe to support a person in the water.

LIFEJACKET Waistcoat or jacket with integral buoyancy to support a person in the water. An 'Approved' lifejacket will keep the victim on his back with his head above the water.

LIFELINE A line attached to a safety harness with which crew can secure himself to a boat. One of the lines forming the guardrails round a boat.

LIFERAFT An inflatable circular raft with a canopy which must be of a size to support and protect the full crew.

LOG The instrument for measuring distance and speed through the water. The complete record of a passage or voyage.

LONGITUDE Meridians, lines which pass through both poles. There are 180° of longitude east and west of the Greenwich Meridian, which is 0°. Position is measured by degrees east or west of the Greenwich Meridian, and the latitude north or south of the equator.

LUFF The leading edge of a sail. To luff up is to put the helm down and bring the head of a boat into the wind.

LUG. LUGSAIL A quadrilateral shaped sail attached to a spar which is hoisted up the mast and hung at an acute angle to leeward with its tack forward of the mast.

LWL Load Waterline. The length of a boat at her waterline when loaded to her correct design displacement.

MAGNETIC BEARING The bearing of an object or course related to the position of magnetic north, as opposed to true or geographical north.

MAGNETIC COURSE A direction read from a magnetic compass. The true course worked out on a chart with variation added or subtracted to convert it to magnetic so that a compass course can be steered.

MAINSAIL The sail hoisted on the largest or main mast.

MAINSHEET The rope tackle used to haul in or ease out the boom to trim the mainsail.

MAKE FAST Belay a rope. Secure a boat.

MAKE HEADWAY Make progress through the water.

MAKING A tide is making when flooding or coming
in.

MARCONI RIG The American term for bermudan
rig.

MARK Any object or sign used for guiding or giving
warning to shipping.

MAST A vertical spar on which sails are set.

MASTHEAD RIG A fore-and-aft rig with the
forestay going to the top of the mast.

MIZZEN A fore-and-aft sail set on a smaller mizzen
mast at or near the stern. Also called a spanker
(American), but never a mizzen sail.

MOORINGS A series of anchors or heavy weights
with chains in a harbour, estuary or sheltered waters
to which boats can make fast. An anchorage is an
area where the shelter and the ground are suitable
for boats to lie to their own anchors. There may
also be moorings in the same area. When a boat is
tied up alongside she is said to be 'moored up', not
at a mooring.

MOTOR SAILER A boat designed and engined for
cruising and passage making as much, if not more,
under power than sail. Motor sailing means using
the engine while still sailing if in a hurry or to stem
a foul tide if the wind is not good enough.

NAUTICAL MILE A distance equal to 1/60th of a
degree of latitude. 6,080 ft or 1·8532 km.

NEAP TIDES Those with a smaller range than spring
tides. Neaps occur at half moon periods both
waxing and waning.

NOTICES TO MARINERS Notifications published
periodically for making corrections to charts.

OBSERVED POSITION A boat's position deduced
from observation of navigational and/or land marks.

OFFSHORE Away from the coast. Out of sight of
land.

OFFSHORE WIND A wind blowing from the land.

OFF THE WIND Any point of sailing which is not
close hauled. Applies especially when the wind is
abaft the beam and the sails are eased well out.

ONSHORE WIND A wind blowing towards the
land.

OUTHAUL A rope or tackle used to extend the foot
of a sail.

OVERFALLS Rough or confused water caused by the
tidal stream running over a very rough bottom or
sudden changes in depths.

OVERHANG Of bow or stern beyond the waterline
length.

PAINTER A light mooring rope attached to the bow
of a tender or small boat.

PAY OFF Turn downwind, to leeward.

PEAK The top outer point of a gaff sail.

PINCH Sail too close to the wind and lose speed.

PITCH The fore-and-aft seesaw movement of a boat

in a rough sea or swell.

POINT To point well is to sail well close to the wind.

PORT The left hand side of a boat looking forward. A
harbour.

PORT TACK A boat is sailing on the port tack when
the wind is coming from the port hand side.

POSITION LINE Line on a chart deduced from
taking a bearing or sounding and along which the
boat is therefore known to be. Two position lines
make a fix at their point of intersection.

PREVENTER A line attached to the end of a boom
or spar and secured forward to prevent it from
swinging about in rolling sea conditions.

PULPIT A metal railing round the bow of a boat to
protect the crew when working on the foredeck.

PUSHPIT Similar to a pulpit, but fixed round the
stern or aft deck.

QUARTER The aft corners of a boat. Wind on the
quarter would be blowing over one corner or the
other.

RACE An area of very turbulent water caused by a
strong current or tidal stream accelerating round a
headland or through a narrows. Sometimes caused
by the configuration of the sea bed. Apart from the
discomfort and possible danger of the turbulence, it
is often impossible to sail against the strength of a
race. Going with the stream a boat might be carried
along out of control.

RAFTING Two or more boats mooring alongside
each other.

RANGE The difference between the height of high
and low water of one tide. The distance at which a
light can be seen.

REACH The point of sailing when the wind is
coming from the beam. On a beam reach it is
roughly at right angles to the boat, on a fine reach a
little ahead of the beam, and on a broad reach a
little abaft the beam.

READY ABOUT Warning given when about to
tack.

REEF Reduce the amount of sail carried by folding,
rolling or tying up part of a sail. An alternative to
changing to smaller sails when the wind is too
strong. A chain of rocks just below the surface of the
water.

REEF KNOT Used to tie two ropes together.

REEF POINTS Short lengths of line sewn in rows on
each side of a sail for tying up the part of a sail that
has been reefed.

RESERVE BUOYANCY Extra buoyancy by way of
watertight compartments, cans or inflatable bags
which will keep a capsized or waterlogged boat
afloat.

RIG The sail, mast and rigging plan of a boat.

RIGGING The general term for all wires and ropes

that support spars, and those used to hoist, lower and trim sails. The former is standing rigging, the latter running rigging.

ROLLER REEFING A method of reefing or furling sails by rolling them round a boom or furling spar.

ROUND TURN AND TWO HALF HITCHES A knot used to secure a rope or line by taking a turn round an object and then taking two half hitches round the standing part of that rope.

ROVE Describes a rope passed through an eye or block.

RUDDER A hinged flat on or near the stern by which a boat is steered.

RUNNING Sailing with the wind aft.

RUNNING FIX A boat's position plotted by taking two bearings on one object with an interval between.

SAMPSON POST A strong post on the foredeck or aft deck of a boat to which mooring lines or anchor cable can be secured.

SCHOONER A fore-and-aft rigged boat with two or more masts. A big boat rig most suitable for long reaches in trade wind parts of the world.

SEIZED Bound with wire, line or twine.

SET The direction of flow of a tidal stream. To set sail is to hoist sail. To sail off.

SHANK The long arm or middle part of an anchor.

SHEETS Ropes secured to the clew of a sail to control it.

SHOAL An area of water which is very shallow and a hazard.

SHROUDS Standing rigging which supports a mast on either side.

SKEG An extension of the keel, or a separate embryonic keel which carries the hinged length of a rudder.

SLOOP Fore-and-aft rigged boat with only two sails, main and head.

SLOT The gap forming a venturi between a headsail and the leeward side of a mainsail.

SNATCH BLOCK A block with a hinged side which opens to take a rope without having to rove it through.

SNUB Check a line or chain from running out, usually by taking a turn round a cleat or post.

SPAR General term for masts, booms, poles, gaffs, etc.

SPLICE Join two wires or ropes by intertwining their strands.

SPONSONS The outer hulls of a trimaran. The side tubes of an inflatable boat.

SPREADER or CROSSTREE Strut at right angles to the mast to tension the shrouds, and hold them out to provide a wider angle of attack so providing better support.

SPRING TIDES Those with the highest range. Springs occur at the full and new moon periods.

SQUARESAIL A four-sided sail rigged on a yard at right angles to the mast.

STANCHIONS Upright supports for guardrails or lifelines round the sides of a boat.

STANDING RIGGING All rigging which is permanently set up to support masts, as opposed to running rigging which hoists and controls sails.

STARBOARD The right hand side of a boat when looking forward, opposite of port.

STARBOARD TACK A boat is sailing on the starboard tack when the wind is coming from the starboard hand side.

STAY Wire or rope supporting a mast in the fore or aft direction.

STAYSAIL A sail set up on a stay. Sometimes it is set flying secured only at head, tack and clew.

STEERAGE WAY Enough movement through the water to enable a rudder to be effective and a boat to be steered.

STERN The aft part of a boat.

STERNWAY The movement of a boat going astern. To make sternway is intentional. To make a sternboard is to fall away astern because of wind or tide.

STOCK The cross piece at the upper end of the shank of an anchor. It is set at right angles to the arms and flukes so that they do not lie flat on the bottom.

SWAGE See 'swigging'.

SWIGGING Getting a purchase on a rope by pulling on the standing part as one would a bow string and then quickly hauling on the tail to take up the slack gained.

TACK The lower fore corner of a sail by which it is attached to a boom, deck, stemhead or bowsprit. It keeps the luff amidships. To tack is to go about, change direction.

TACKLE A system of rope and blocks (pulleys) to provide a gain in purchase for hoisting or hauling.

TAIL To haul on a rope which has one or more turns round a winch.

TENDER A small boat used as a ferry boat, sometimes lifeboat, to a bigger boat. Can also describe a boat which needs little wind to make her heel. The opposite is a stiff boat which requires a strong wind to make her heel.

THROAT The upper fore corner of a gaff sail formed by the angle of the head and the luff.

THWART Bench seat across the width of a boat.

TIDAL STREAM The movement caused by the rise and fall of tides. Its direction and rate of movement are predictable.

TIDE The perpetual rise and fall of the oceans and seas caused by the changing gravitational pull of the moon and sun resulting in an ebb and flow of water.

TIERS Canvas strips or short cords for securing sail when furled. Shock cords with plastic connectors or elastic loops with balls are now more commonly used for speed and convenience.

TILLER A wood or metal bar fixed to the rudder head to afford a lever by which to move and hold the rudder steady and so steer the boat.

TOE RAIL A low rail or miniature bulwark running round the sides of the deck.

TOPPING LIFT A rope or wire used to raise or lower a spar. Most commonly used for the main boom to take the weight when the sail is being lowered and when it is furled.

TOPSIDES That part of the hull of a boat which is above water.

TRANSIT When two objects are visually in line they are said to be in transit.

TRANSOM Flat or shaped piece across the aft end of a hull. The back side of a boat.

TRAVELLER A fitting which can travel along or up a spar or track.

TRICK A spell at the helm.

TRIP THE ANCHOR Break it out of the ground.

TROTS A system of mooring buoys or piles laid out in line. Boats use fore and aft mooring lines and so do not swing with the tide but remain in line.

UNDER SAIL Moving under sail with no engine running.

UNDER WAY Moving under control.

UP HELM Put the tiller to windward to make the head bear away to leeward.

VARIATION The difference between true and magnetic north which varies from year to year and from one part of the world to another. The information to work out current variation is given on charts.

VEER Change direction, most often applied to the wind when it changes direction clockwise. When it goes anti-clockwise it is said to back. Pay out a chain or rope.

VENTURI EFFECT When mainsail and headsail are correctly sheeted in the slot between them accelerates the passage of air over the lee side of the mainsail and cuts down turbulence. This lowers the pressure on the lee side of the mainsail and gives it more drive.

WATCH The crew on duty. The period of time when they are on duty. On watch is on duty, off watch is resting.

WAY Movement through the water.

WEATHER HELM A tendency to turn head to wind which is corrected by putting the tiller up wind to turn the head away from the wind. A boat with pronounced weather helm is badly balanced and very tiring to steer.

WEATHER SIDE The windward or up wind side. The side from which the wind is blowing.

WEIGH ANCHOR Pull the anchor up.

WHISKER POLE A small spar used to hold the clew of a headsail out when running in light airs to prevent the sail collapsing. Mostly used when goosewinged.

WINCH A device with a rotating drum round which a rope is turned to gain a mechanical advantage. By means of gearing inside the drum, and a long handle giving good leverage, enormous purchases can be achieved.

WIND True wind is that felt on shore, or when a boat is stationary. Apparent wind is the sum of the true wind and the wind caused by a boat's own movement.

WIND OVER TIDE When the wind blows in the opposite direction to the set of the tidal stream and the water gets roughed up. When the wind is strong and the tide flows fast heavy seas can build up. In shallow waters the sea becomes steep and confused.

WINDWARD Towards the wind.

YACHTMASTER'S CERTIFICATE A certificate of competence issued jointly by the Royal Yachting Association and the Department of Trade in the UK. It is the highest certificate awarded to amateur skippers.

YARD Spar from which a square sail is hung.

YAW Weave from side to side. Continually go off course, first one way and then the other.

YAWL A two-masted boat with the shorter (mizzen) mast stepped abaft the rudder post or on the stern itself. The mizzen is usually set out over the stern.

ZENITH That point in the sky which is exactly overhead. The highest point to which the sun or other heavenly body rises in the sky.

Index